Psychoanalysis and the Artistic Creation

This book explores the phenomenon of creativity and creation from a psychoanalytic point of view, focusing on understanding the psycho-emotional dynamics underlying artistic creative activities, such as theatre, literature, and painting.

Throughout, Delgado considers these works of art through a Bionian, Kleinian, and Freudian lens. He uses three major psychoanalytic models of the creative process, two of them classic: the first, Freudian, based on the theory of conflict between impulse and defense, the result of the effort to manage an excessive drive activity, and in which the concept of sublimation is central; the second, Kleinian, based on the attachment theory, in which creative effort corresponds to an attempt to repair the damage done to the object or to the self; and the third, more recent, affiliated with the more expanded attachment relationship theory, based on W. Bion's theory of thinking, and emphasizing the continent's capacity for psyche and the oscillation between schizo-paranoid and depressive positions.

With illustrations throughout, this book will be vital reading for anyone interested in the intersection of creativity, the Arts, and psychoanalysis.

Luís Manuel Romano Delgado is a professor at the Institute of Psychology, University Institute (ISPA-IU), Lisbon, Portugal and a psychoanalyst in private practice in Lisbon, and a Full and Training Member of the Portuguese Association of Psychoanalysis and Psychotherapy (APPPP), Portugal, federated in the International Federation of Psychoanalytic Societies (IFPS). He is a Full Member of the Applied Psychology Research Center Capabilities & Inclusion (APPsyCI), which provides investigations of psychology and social problems. His great interest lies in the study of psychodynamics of creativity and psychoanalysis applied to artistic and literary objects. He has published two books on this subject and several articles in national and international journals.

Routledge Focus on Mental Health

Routledge Focus on Mental Health presents short books on current topics, linking in with cutting-edge research and practice.

For a full list of titles in this series, please visit https://www.routledge.com/Routledge-Focus-on-Mental-Health/book-series/RFMH

Psychoanalysis and the Act of Artistic Creation

A Look at the Unconscious Dynamics of Creativity

Luís Manuel Romano Delgado

Routledge
Taylor & Francis Group

LONDON AND NEW YORK

First published 2023
by Routledge
4 Park Square, Milton Park, Abingdon, Oxon OX14 4RN

and by Routledge
605 Third Avenue, New York, NY 10158

Routledge is an imprint of the Taylor & Francis Group, an informa business

© 2023 Luís Manuel Romano Delgado

British Library Cataloguing-in-Publication Data
A catalogue record for this book is available from the British Library

Library of Congress Cataloging-in-Publication Data
Names: Delgado, Luís Manuel Romano, author.
Title: Psychoanalysis and the act of artistic creation : a look at the unconscious
dynamics of creativity / Luís Manuel Romano Delgado.
Description: Abingdon, Oxon ; New York, NY : Routledge, 2023. |
Includes bibliographical references and index. |
Identifiers: LCCN 2022028287 (print) | LCCN 2022028288 (ebook) |
ISBN 9781032340586 (hardback) | ISBN 9781032358581 (paperback) |
ISBN 9781003329015 (ebook)
Subjects: LCSH: Creative ability. | Creation (Literary, artistic, etc.) |
Psychoanalysis and art.
Classification: LCC BF408 .D4457 2023 (print) | LCC BF408 (ebook) |
DDC 153.3/5--dc23/eng/20220815
LC record available at https://lccn.loc.gov/2022028287
LC ebook record available at https://lccn.loc.gov/2022028288

ISBN: 978-1-032-34058-6 (hbk)
ISBN: 978-1-032-35858-1 (pbk)
ISBN: 978-1-003-32901-5 (ebk)

DOI: 10.4324/9781003329015

Typeset in Times New Roman
by Deanta Global Publishing Services, Chennai, India

To my students, to Solange and to Martim

Contents

Book presentation

This book, in the form of eight articles corresponding to oral interventions by Luís Manuel Romano Delgado in national and international forums of the specialty, focuses on the phenomenon of creativity and creation from the psychoanalytic point of view. More precisely, the effort focuses on understanding the psycho-emotional dynamics underlying artistic creative activity in its various manifestations: theater, literature, painting, etc.

It is a work of extra-therapeutic (extra-clinical) psychoanalysis, applied to the domains of human activity that constitute the intellectual and artistic productions, which, like Freud, along with an interest in the collective functioning (social and political), considers psychoanalysis of cultural objects as a priority field for psychoanalysis.

From a theoretical point of view, the originality of this work lies in the use and application of various models or psychoanalytic theories in the understanding of some creative processes in the artistic field. We fundamentally used three major psychoanalytic models of the creative process, two of them classic: the first, Freudian, based on the theory of the conflict between impulse and defense, the result of the effort to manage an excessive drive activity, and in which the concept of sublimation is central; the second, Kleinian, based on the attachment theory, in which creative effort corresponds to an attempt to repair the damage done to the object or to the self; and the third, more recent, affiliated with the more expanded attachment relationship theory, based on W. Bion's theory of thinking and emphasizing the continent's capacity for psyche and the oscillation between schizo-paranoid and depressive positions; we have not forgotten Winnicott's contributions of transitional space and object and Arietti's contributions to the tertiary processes of thought.

In the present work, the reader will have access to relevant and stimulating illustrated and illustrative examples, which are not meant to lighten or beautify, but to be carriers of information as iconographic texts to read.

Theoretical introduction[1]

The technique of psychological investigation created by Freud added a new dimension to human sciences: unconscious psychodynamics. Psychoanalysis applied to artistic creativity refers back to the psychoanalytic knowledge that is willing to face and understand the hidden side that provides a tone of mystery to artistic creation.

The essence of our theme refers to the dynamics of the creative faculty as representing the higher link of a constellation of psycho-emotional processes active in any type of creation, whether scientific or artistic, with special emphasis on the latter, since, in the former, the control of the conscious ego is much more intense, while in the latter, these processes are incomparably freer in terms of the fluctuation of meaning and the emotional coloring of images and words.

Psychoanalysts are unanimous in indicating the existence of two states in our mental life: one related to wakefulness, where attention is focused on the world of external reality, and the other, oneiric, directed to the internal reality and which is always active, whether the subject is awake or asleep. And it is this dream life that is associated with the aesthetic and creative aspects of mental life, the creator being the one who, mastering the technique, manages, in the most efficient way possible, to rescue the thoughts and images that emotional experiences have left behind in their fleeting passage through the mind.

We can conceive psychoanalysis as a huge, coherent architectural complex, but made up of several theoretical models that interpenetrate, complement, and complete each other, always maintaining an openness to new models. In the present work, we selected the authors whose theories or models of thought seem fundamental in this domain of understanding the psycho-emotional dynamics underlying the processes of artistic creativity and creation. First Freud, Klein, and Bion, followed by Winnicott and

---

1 For a container whose contents were dispersed.

Arietti. We will focus on the construction and development of the ability to *symbolize* and produce thoughts, as these are what make you think and, furthermore, develop the *thinking apparatus*, the basis of creativity and creation – although not all creatives are capable of taking the leap towards creation – artistic creation is the symbol par excellence.

In Sigmund Freud's conception, the topic that interests us is *sublimation*, which plays the most significant role in the defense mechanisms available to the ego in its permanent effort to adapt and survive in civilized life. More than a defense mechanism, it is this process that allows cultural, scientific, and ideological activity to be carried out without conflict, that is, freed from conflicting ties that would unite it to instinctual fantasies and childhood conflicts (Freud, 1910/1981).

On the other hand, Freud (1907/1981) compares artistic activity to children's dreaming and playing, and these are activities that have repression and the disguised fulfillment of desire in common. The essence of artistic activity consists not in the representation of what really exists, but in masking reality. Further on, we can see an interesting illustration regarding the creation of Picasso's painting, *Les Demoiselles d'Avignon* (1907).

The modifications introduced by Freud (1914/1982) with the established relationship between sublimation and narcissism emphasize part of the powerful motives that the creator derives from their activity: narcissistic gratification.

Based on the two processes of psychic functioning described by Freud (1911/1981), and taking into account the relationship between symbolism and the two psychic processes, it seems interesting and enriching to include the thought of Silvano Arietti (1976), in which the mechanisms of the primary process reappear in the creative process in strange and intricate combinations, together with the mechanisms of the secondary process, in unpredictable syntheses, having proposed the concept of a *tertiary process* to designate such a special combination. This process would combine the worlds of matter, the psychic and external reality, and, often, the rational and the irrational. The formal aspect of the aesthetic experience depends on that particular combination. In Art and Literature, the primary process is enriching with its contents, while the secondary orders and contains. We will present an illustration of the *tertiary process* later on, in connection with the canvas *I and the Village* by Marc Chagall (1911).

In Donald Winnicott's (1971/1975) opinion, the origin of creativity is in transitional objects, through the establishment of an intermediate area between reality and illusion, called *potential space*. The existence of this space is of the highest importance for development, for experience and, above all, for creative cultural life. Winnicott claims that this space can be considered a third area of human life, not entirely individual (self) nor entirely belonging to the world of separate reality (non-self). Potential space is thus situated between the self and the non-self, between inner and outer reality. It is in the *potential space* that, if the individual has enough confidence in their surroundings, they can explore the interaction between themselves and the world, and can create imaginative transformations of the world, that is, cultural products with symbolic value that can be appreciated by others.

If, for Winnicott, *play* is the paradigm of cultural activity, then the *transitional object* is the paradigm of the work of art. Let us not forget, as we saw earlier, that in Freud's thought art was already situated halfway between reality and imagination. Brilliantly, he compared the artist's creation to the child's play. This one, with their toy, is creating! The artist will continue to play throughout their adult life, through their imagination. Regarding the canvas *I and the Village* (Chagall) we also have an illustration of the potential space.

For Melanie Klein, with her *reparation* theory (1926/1996), the conception of human creativity is understood as a reparative event in a drama linked to the image of the mother or the parents. For her, reparation is linked to the *depressive position* (1930/1996), that is, the moment of weaning and separation, when the child recognizes the mother as a total object, and when their capabilities of symbolic transformation of objects allow them to face the absence of the primary object. In this way, the forming of the symbol appears linked to the experiences of frustration and separation. The child's ability to elaborate these facts will be essential to their ability to organize symbolic thinking and language itself. This magical moment of the evolutionary age is considered the peak of human creativity. The artistic creativity that appears later in adulthood would only represent the transformation of this type of emotion and fantasy experienced in childhood. As Klein's direct disciple Hinshelwood clearly states, "Separation is the strongest element of constructive and creative impulses" (1991/1992, p. 279).

Within the Kleinian theory of reparation, we cannot fail to mention the existence of the divergent opinion of Chasseguet-Smiergel (1984), according to which the deep objective of a creative activity is the *repair of the self* that is felt as damaged, and not of the object itself. Later on, we will illustrate and comment on some types of artistic activity of a repairing nature, including Frida Kahlo's canvas, *The Broken Column* (1944).

We will delve in more detail into the fundamental aspects of Wilfred Bion's *theory of thinking*, as he is the last great innovative psychoanalyst author, not yet fully divulged, and for being the most used in the manuscripts that follow.

Later, with Bion, we witness a profound theoretical transformation of the origins and development of thought and the creative process in relation to the model proposed by Klein. If, for the latter, the *primum movens* of symbolization, of the organization of thought, and of creative activity is situated in the guilt (and/or fear of retaliation) of the damage/destruction of the parents, for Bion (1962/1991) it is the frustration due to the absence of the breast that promotes the organization of *the apparatus to symbolize and think*.

First, we must always bear in mind the concept of *alpha dream work*: something that is located in the human being's mind as it functions, whether during the day or at night, and has to do with unconscious fantasy. It is a mental process and is the representational counterpart that all facts have in psychic reality. There are these fantasies that the creator has more possibilities of assessing. We found that Bion's theories about the *alpha function* and the *continent function* for the psyche are part of the three main psychoanalytic models utilized here, and prove to be extremely important for understanding why the most capable subjects for creative achievement are also the most apt, either for the *sublimatory derivation* or for the *depressive elaboration*. Indeed, the role of the *alpha function* is essential in creativity insofar as it is responsible for recording and elaborating the sensory and emotional data experienced, the *beta elements*, leading them to consciousness before the activation of repression or projection–evacuation. But these processes are only possible due to the active presence of the *container function*.

There is symbolization when the loved object is present internally, even in its physical absence. Recall that this model is already implicit in Freud (1907/1981) insofar as, for him, ideation and thought only exist when instinctual satisfaction is disturbed, when the object of desire is not present. Freud stated that the satisfied man does not fantasize, only the dissatisfied. Eugenio Montale poetically states the same: "Only isolated people speak, only isolated people communicate [...] others repeat, echo" (2004, p. 31). For Bion (1963), thinking is a personality function (*alpha function*) in continuous development and transformation, containing, like Klein, reparative goals.

Thus, the real creative factor lies in the fact that certain personalities can not only handle all those elements and organize them, but also, and above all, open themselves to the unexplored (doubt, uncertainty, mystery ...), and be able to support and tolerate it. The creative artist is someone who seeks and has the ability to contain certain sensations, emotions, and thoughts without becoming disorganized, and expressing them aesthetically.

We have just spoken about the *container's capacity* for the psyche, which seems to constitute one of the fundamental psychic conditions that allow for the creative artistic psycho-emotional dynamic, insofar as it guarantees these phenomena of *regression at the service of the ego*, in the words of the psychoanalyst and art historian Ernst Kris (1952/1965); that is, the relaxation of the conscious control of the ego (controlled regression), allowing communication with other, more primary levels of consciousness, that is, with other forms of perception, sensitivity, and thought, as well as allowing for the freedom of the path and coexistence of psychic contents of different natures, from the most chaotic and instinctual to the most organized and 'sublime', and also the stabilization of turbulent and painful psycho-emotional processes, so that a new and original idea can develop and that, in the expansive impetus, is not destroyed. In Bionian terms, the *containing capacity* is developed by the child's assimilation of the mother's *capacity to reverie* in her relationship with them: the capacity to receive, contain, transform, and return the child's projection–evacuations.

For Bion (1963), the creative effort, especially on the artistic plane, is seen as a process, on a small scale, of small oscillations between the fragment and the whole, of balancing between the paranoid–schizoid position and the depressive position, having represented this process with the *PS<—>D* symbol. The subject, in their creative process, can take advantage of these useful oscillations from a cognitive point of view, as they are the balance between *divergent thinking*, characterized by the creation of logical alternatives, and therefore original, and *convergent thinking*, characterized by the creation of logical needs. It is through the balanced oscillation between these two modes of thinking (dispersive and integrative) or, in classical terms, of the primary and secondary processes, that *creative flexibility* is produced (Kubie, 1958). The presence of this process is extremely clear in James Joyce's writing and in the Cubist phase of Pablo Picasso's paintings, as we can see in some of the following manuscripts.

A note with regard to the deep *issue* of the creator that drives them to the creation of the work.

There are several products of creation: writing, the visual arts, dance, architecture, theater … and the final work is, very often, the result of an inner process mobilized by a need to resolve or, at least, appease an internal psychological distress (Schmid-Kitsikis, 1999, p. 27).

We can say, according to the theories exposed above, that the problem of the creator rests on the *object lost* or damaged by the subject (from the perspective of repairing the depressive position), or on the *lost phallus* (from the perspective of castration, through the reconstitution of a whole and phallic body), and there is always an attempt at *reparation* or *narcissistic gratification*.

Chasseguet-Smirgel analyzes the importance of the therapeutic repercussions of the creative act, in that it allows the subject a narcissistic recovery without external intervention. Let's listen to it: "In this sense, creation is a self-creation, and the creative act draws its deep impulse from the desire to alleviate, by its own means, the gaps left or caused by others" (1984, p. 102).

Some illustrations:

The case of the writer Marguerite Duras, for whom the pain of successive losses and the loneliness of the voids left along the way, led her to find, through literary production, the conditions to continue living. Wasn't she the one who said "writing a novel is solving a crisis"? I would add "the need to write continuously".

Or the case, as we will see later, of the Mexican painter Frida Kahlo who, after an accident that severely damaged her body and caused her permanent physical pain as well as a deep narcissistic wound, found relief in monothematic painting, the representation of herself. In the space of absolute bodily pain, she is alone, in her entirety, the deserted soul, in which what still survives is her art in the ability to express what is not possible otherwise, the need to show, without words, the visible of unspeakable suffering.

The philosopher Søren Kierkegaard, with a pain of the soul, of existing, of the restlessness of the despair in which he plunged, wanting to find answers to existential absurdity, searching in religion and writing for a way to bear the faith and doubt that afflicted him.

Also António Lobo Antunes, a Portuguese writer who, in an interesting interview with George Steiner, clearly confesses that "suicide is something that has been with me since an early age. I had a series of very serious illnesses as a child, but there was always a self-destructive tendency in me. What always saved me was writing".

References

Arietti, S. (1976). *Creativity: The magic synthesis*. New York: Basic Books, Inc. Publishers.
Bion, W. (1962/1991). Uma teoria do pensar [A theory of thinking]. In Elizabeth Bott Spillius (Ed.), *Melanie Klein hoje* (Vol. 1, pp. 185–193). Rio-de-Janeiro: Imago.
Bion, W. (1963). *The elements of psychoanalysis*. London: Heineman.
Chasseguet-Smirgel, J. (1977). *Pour une psychanalyse de l'arte et de la créativité*. [For a psychoanalysis of art and creativity]. Paris: P.B.P.
Freud, S. (1907/1981). El poeta y los sueños diurnos [Creative writers and daydreaming]. In *Sigmund Freud, Obras Completas* (Tomo II, pp. 1343–1348). Madrid: Biblioteca Nueva.
Freud, S. (1910/1981). Un recuerdo infantil de Leonardo de Vinci [A childhood memory of Leonardo de Vinci]. In *Sigmund Freud, Obras Completas* (Tomo II, pp. 1579–1619]. Madrid: Biblioteca Nueva.
Freud, S. (1911/1981). Los dos princípios del funcionamiento mental [Two principles of mental functioning]. In *Sigmund Freud, Obras Completas* (Tomo II, pp. 1638–1642). Madrid: Biblioteca Nueva.
Freud, S. (1914/1982). Pour introduir le narcissisme [On narcissisme: An introduction]. In *Sigmund Freud, La vie sexuelle* (pp. 11–14). Paris: Presses Universitaires de France.

Hinshelwood, R. D. (1991/1992). *Dicionário do pensamento Kleiniano* [A dictionary of Kleinian thought]. Porto Alegre: Artes Médicas.

Klein, M. (1926/1996). Princípios psicológicos da análise de crianças pequenas [Psychological principles of young children analysis]. In *Melanie Klein, Amor, culpa e reparação* (pp. 153–163). Rio-de-Janeiro: Imago.

Klein, M. (1930/1996). A importância da formação de símbolos no desenvolvimento do ego [The importance of symbol formation in ego development]. In *Melanie Klein – Amor, Culpa e Reparação* (pp. 251–264). Rio-de-janeiro: Imago.

Kris, E. (1952/1965). *Psychoanalytic exploration in art*. New York: International University Press.

Kubie, L. S. (1958). *Neurotic distortion of the creative process*. Lawrence: University of Kansas.

Schmid-Kitsikis, E. (1999). Ancrage identitaire. Destins des créateurs [Identity anchoring. Destinies of creators]. *Revue Française de Psychanalyse, 4*(Tome XIII), 1212–1225.

Winnicott, D. (1971/1975). *Jeu et réalité, l'espace potentiel* [Playing and reality, potential space]. Paris: Gallimard.

1 Freudian sublimation in artistic creation

Prehistory of the term

Millennia of efforts have taken Man to isolate that pure psychic intimacy felt within ourselves. The formation of personal pronouns tells the story of this effort and shows how the idea of how "I" was formed, in a slow ebb, from the most external to the most internal. In place of "I", we first used the words "my flesh", "my body", "my heart", "my chest". We, by pronouncing with some emphasis "I", still support the hand on the sternum, in a gesture that is a residue of the subject's old body notion. Man begins to know himself by the things that belong to him. The possessive pronoun precedes the persona.

In this beautiful text by Ortega y Gasset (1946/1993, p. 334) we see the very slow and decisive work of constructive sublimation/symbolization of the human being, in the broad sense of the term, as there is a purification of the elements and purely and exclusively physical experiences, solid, palpable, in more abstract and psychological elements.

The term *sublimation* originally designates a material purification and, in alchemical practices, the process of purifying a body's purge in its heterogeneous parts, through fire; in the material domain, it is intended to achieve the transmutation of base metals into gold and silver, noble metals.

As Anzieu (1979) tells us, even before psychoanalysis, the term *sublimation*, through a metaphorical derivation, was transposed to the domain of moral purification; the sexual drive purifies itself of its biological components, linked to the reproduction of the species, to reach higher targets of an aesthetic, intellectual, ethical, religious, cultural nature, with a civilizing value.

DOI: 10.4324/9781003329015-1

Sublimation: definition

From the moment that we propose to question the nature of the creative process that leads to the creation of cultural objects, we can question, in relation to the individuals who indulge in the creative process, that is, who produce innovative work of recognized quality, in which measure they are able to derive their drive energy in sublimated activities and in which fields of interests. We consider creative activity to come out of sublimation processes and Freud's thinking about sublimation is very explicit, in that it specifically states that artistic and intellectual creation is clearly located in the sublimation field.

We use the definition proposed by Laplanche and Pontalis:

> Sublimation: a process postulated by Freud to explain human activities that have no apparent relationship to sexuality, but that would find their driving element in the force of the sexual drive. Freud described as sublimation mainly artistic activities and intellectual investigation. It is said that the drive is sublimated insofar as it is derived for a new non-sexual target and insofar as it targets socially valued objects.
>
> (1967/1970, pp. 637–638)

Sublimation in Freud

Freud's texts do not allow for an establishment of a true theory of sublimation, as this notion has never been the subject of a specific text: it is treated in a certain number of works without, however, being deepened.

The term first appears in *Three Essays on the Theory of Sexuality* (Freud, 1905/1975), with sublimation being treated as one of the three ways out of childhood sexuality, the other two being perversion and neurosis. It is a process that characterizes "normal functioning, and which intervenes during the latency period, by transforming infantile sexuality [from pre-genital sexual energy] at the expense of the child's sexual tendencies" (p. 187). However, the domain of sublimation is not available to everyone: "Only a minority does it, and moreover intermittently and with much more difficulty during the period of youthful ardor" (Freud, 1908/1982, p. 38).

Freud (1908/1981) develops a line of a reasoning in which he identifies as a base and motor of the highest human achievement a force originated from what would be the lowest and most threatening social point of view, that is, the perverse–polymorphous sexuality. The final result of the processes of sublimation during Freud's time would be a direct correlate of a form of social regulation in that nothing differs from the defense mechanism of repression, and in this way rather than the man's spiritual elevation, the fate of such desexualizations would be just the final installation of the discontent in culture.

Sublimation is an essential concept of the theoretical edifice of psychoanalysis that nevertheless remains incoherent and underdeveloped. In 1929, Freud wrote in *Civilization and Its Discontents*:

> satisfactions of this order, for example, that the artist finds in creation or feels when embodying the images of his fantasy, or that the thinker finds in solving a problem or in discovery of the truth, have a particular quality that one day we will be able to characterize in a metapsychological manner.
>
> (1929/1981, p. 3027)

The only in-depth study in relation to which all those who try to analyze sublimation in Freud's work are led to, is the study of a great creator, Leonardo da Vinci (Freud, 1910/1982), which nevertheless poses problems when it comes to generalizing hypotheses regarding its functioning to a population without artistic gifts.

Theory of support

During an initial period, Freud promoted the theory of support for sexual drives in self-preservation drives to consider the way in which the sublimation process works, that is, the deviation from sexual to non-sexual. Examining what is happening in relation to the object and the target in the support, Freud notes that the transition from self-preservation to sexuality introduces a phantomization movement: "from a factual, material relationship, the ingestion of milk, we move to a phantasmatic relationship and transposable to many others, such as the incorporation of the omnipotent breast" (Laplanche, 1975/1977, p. 61).

In conclusion, we can claim that sublimation is part of this relationship between the two planes – self-conservation and sexuality.

The passage of libido through the ego

The changes introduced by Freud to psychoanalytic theory with the intro-duction of the concept of narcissism (Freud, 1914/1981) and then with the death instinct, will lead him to modify his point of view in relation to sub-limation. In *The Ego and the Id* (1923/1981), Freud introduces the idea that the process of sublimation operates through a retraction in the self of sexual libido, a retraction that allows for a desexualization of it: "The trans-formation we witnessed here, of the libidinous attitude towards the object in a narcissistic libido, evidently implies the renunciation of purely sexual targets, a desexualization, thus a kind of sublimation" (Freud, 1923/1981, p. 2725).

Kris, in his beautiful book *Psychoanalytical Exploration in Art* (1952/1965), doesn't consider art–aesthetic as an expression of repressed instinctual conflict. On the contrary, he developed the idea of artistic sublimation as a mature form of defense which neutralized potentially dangerous drive energies and made them available to the ego. The artist, through "regression in the service of the ego", enabled the aesthetic illusion from which neutralized unconscious could create socially valued objects. This successor to Freud rethought art as an important aspect of the ego's adaptation to the environment.

The relationship established by Freud between sublimation and narcissism emphasizes part of the powerful motives that the artist and the creator derive from their activity. In short, and as Anzieu states: "Schematically, it can be considered that the creator replaces direct sexual satisfaction with narcissistic gratification. It is of paramount importance for himself, certainly, but also for culture" (1979, p. 32).

The target

The target of the drive, in the *Three Essays on the Theory of Sexuality*, is "the act towards which the drive has a tendency".

The modification of the target of the drive in sublimation was suggested by Freud in the *Three Essays on the Theory of Sexuality*, and it is in *"Civilized" Sexual Morality and Modern Nervous Illness* that he is most clear and decisive:

> The sexual drive […] makes available to cultural work an extraordinary amount of forces, and this is no doubt as a result of its particularly pronounced property in displacing its target without losing essentially in intensity. The capacity to exchange the target that is originally sexual for another that is no longer sexual, but that is psychically related as the first, is called sublimation capacity.
>
> (Freud, 1908/1981, p. 2025)

This modification can be interpreted in the following way: from a biological breeding target, one moves to a culturally creative target.

The new target (symbol) is psychically related to the first (sexual). Classic example: a voyeuristic (partial) drive whose goal is to satisfy sexual curiosity in relation to female sexual organs will be transformed, sublimated into intellectual interest (target modification) by astronomy (object modification).

We conclude by stating that the phenomenon of sublimation consists of a process of desexualization that leads to a movement of elevation, resulting from the first investments, indicating the subject's possibilities, at a given moment of his development, to mobilize and transform, for different mental constructions, simultaneously his libidinal energy, his psychic modulations (fantasies, symbols, images, etc.) elaborated through his psychosexual history and systems of thought.

Freud and art

Next, we will address Freud's psychoanalytic contribution to the study of art, showing how his general psychological discoveries were valid in fields outside of pathology, especially regarding the relationship between the activity of the creative imagination and the productive capacity of man, and the processes of thought in action.

Perhaps the fundamental way in which Freud approached the vast domain of art was the study of the artist's imagination. "At the beginning of his work, Freud felt that only rigorous scientific thinking could differentiate his approach from that of intuitive psychologists, such as the poets whose works he always admired" (Kris, 1952/1965, p. 25). At the end of his life, when he no longer had any doubt about the autonomous character of the psychoanalytic contribution, he refers to philosophers, writers, and poets as those "to whom he was indebted [...] without having made great efforts, of deep truths, extracted from the whirlwind of their emotions, which we only reach in a painful way, constantly constrained by painful uncertainties" (Freud, 1929/1981, p. 3066).

Freud considered artistic creation to be a part of mental functioning closely related to the formation of dreams. For the inventor of psychoanalysis, creativity was saturated by the conscious elaboration of the residues of everyday experiences, especially those that are repressed by the unconscious. Freud, when discovering the unconscious, became interested in the internal world and the language of the dream and, in many of his writings, he referred to art works. For him, the language of the unconscious is the language of the unrepresentable that is being constructed and reconstructed in an incessant search for the truth. In the opening of his article *Creative Writers and Daydreaming*, he writes:

> We lay people always feel an intense curiosity in knowing from which sources this strange being, the creative writer, extracts his material [...] and how he manages to produce in us such an impression with him and awaken emotions that we may not even think we are capable of.
>
> (Freud, 1907/1981, p. 1343)

6   *Freudian sublimation in artistic creation*

The fascination with this exclusive activity of man led Freud to become interested in the psychobiography of some artists, not as a reconstruction of childhood, but because he believed that the artistic work incorporated the conflicts and unconscious fantasies of its author. So, in the book *Leonardo da Vinci and a Memory of His Childhood* (1910/1981), Freud, using some biographical data, a childhood memory, and two of his paintings: the *Mona Lisa* and *Virgin and Child with Saint Anne*, sought to reconstruct Leonardo's psychosexual development. For Freud, in the smile of Gioconda, Leonardo da Vinci resurrects the expression of his mother's smile and, in *Virgin and Child with Saint Anne*, he integrates the mother and the stepmother, which is also reflected in the pyramidal structure of the painting.

Freud also analyzed some literary works. In *Dostoevsky and Parricide* (1927/1981), Freud does a reading of the universal theme of the Oedipus and parricide complex. In *The Brothers Karamazov*, he describes the split in personality. In other works, Freud approached themes that illustrate universal problems, without directly associating them with a psychobiography of the author. He interprets, for example, Cordelia, in *King Lear* (by Shakespeare), as a symbol of death, and the reconciliation of the characters as a reconciliation with life.

For Freud, art was, above all, an opportunity to fulfill, on the fantasy plane, the desires that real life frustrated, either by external obstacles or by moral inhibitions. In this way, art is conceived as a kind of wildlife reserve in development from the beginning of pleasure to the beginning of reality and, while it creates civilization, it acts as a safety valve protecting civilization. Here are some illustrative excerpts from Freud's works:

> Art gives way to a peculiar reconciliation between the two principles [of pleasure and reality]. The artist is originally a man who distances himself from reality because he cannot accept the renouncement of the satisfaction of the instincts that it shies away from, and a man who allows his erotic and ambitious desires to act fully in his phantasmatic life. Undoubtedly, he finds a way to return from that world of fantasy to reality using special stratagems to mold his fantasies as truths of a new genre that men appreciate as valuable reflections of reality. And, in this way, he becomes, in a way, the hero, the king, the creator, or the favorite he wanted to be, without having to resort to the long and tortuous path that requires him to make changes in the outside world.
>
> (Freud, 1911/1981, p. 1641)

There is only one branch of our civilization in which the omnipotence of thoughts has been preserved, and that branch is art. Only through art does it continue to happen that a man consumed by desires does something similar to the satisfaction of those desires, something that, thanks to the artistic illusion, produces emotional effects as if it were real.

(Freud, 1913/1981, p. 1804)

Genesis of the creation of *Les Demoiselles d'Avignon* (Picasso)

Art critic Leo Steinberg (1972) created a method that he called "*subjective creative archeology*", making us see that the meaning of the work is not what we simply see on the painted canvas, but, above all, the entire creative process that we can rebuild.

Regarding *Les Demoiselles d'Avignon*, it is a work that has gone through a long process of elaboration. An art historian has stated that the hundreds of paintings, drawings, sketches that Picasso produced during the painting's six months of gestation constitute an amount of preparatory work that is not only unique in the artist's career, but also unprecedented across the board in art history. It means that there was an important psychic process in gestation, a sublimatory process.

It started with the idea of a brothel scene. The painting would contain prostitutes, a client, a sailor, or Picasso himself, and it would deal with the fact of seeing (voyeurism), a confrontation with the indestructible demands of sex. From the first preparatory sketches and drawings expressing scenes and characters that were explicitly sexual and almost pornographic, even to the last ones and to the painting itself, there seems to have been a clear moderation in this aspect.

In a reading of the usual content of the painting, we have a brothel in the French city of Avignon, or in the street of Barcelona with the same name. Perhaps some of the naked prostitutes adopt 'professional' postures to stimulate the sexual desire of the client/voyeur, such as raising their arms with their hands behind their heads or sitting on their backsides with their legs wide open, turning their heads to watch someone, or raising the curtain to enter the central area.

The change of the original title of the painting from *Las Putas de la Calle Avignon* to the renowned *Les Demoiselles d'Avignon* is not only related to the morality and business spirit of the *marchant* and the art world. Picasso, with his very active and intense aggressiveness and sexuality, did not know, but his art converged with Freud's discoveries, in the sense that he had proposed the sublimated and symbolized drive as the ultimate engine of creative action.

Figure 1.1 Angel Fernandez de Soto with woman (erotic sketch by Picasso).
Source: Picasso: ©2022, Succession Pablo Picasso, SPA

The importance of this painting, undoubtedly one of the most important of the twentieth century, in addition to all the technical and aesthetic
explanations and interpretations, is perhaps due to the fact that it seeks to
represent the new modern woman, who was to come, with her free body,
aggressive, provocative, master of herself and self-confident. This will be
the great message, the main theme of the work. Do not forget that the female
body of 1907 was covered and imprisoned (the corset would be abolished in
1908!). Everything was going to change. It was this prodigious vision that
Picasso had and represented in this masterpiece.

Thus, genital sexuality would be sublimated and highly symbolized in
the taste element of the fruit tree in front of women: the testicular grapes,
the phallic pear, the vulvar red of the watermelon.

Figure 1.2 Les Demoiselles d'Avignon (Picasso, 1907). Source: Picasso: ©2022, Succession Pablo Picasso, SPA

Two qualities of sublimation

Classical, religious art, with its search for the salvation of humanity, has an ideal that seeks the sublime and transcendence. In the paintings *Saint John the Baptist* by Leonardo da Vinci (1513–1516) and *The Death of Socrates* by Jacques Louis David (1787), the indicator pointing upwards will certainly mean the indication of the path to transcendence in union with the divine or an ethical principle.

Two paintings (*The Restaurant Window* by G. Segal, 1967 and *Just What Is It That Makes Today's Homes So Different, So Appealing* by R. Hamilton, 1965), the first representing two beings without identity, bond, or any ideal, the second representing not a high ideal, but a mere Californian dream in which, to save oneself, it is enough for man to cultivate the material (material comfort, body, sex, music, surfing). In the 'minor art', in which sublimation is imperfect, there is no civilizational effort, looking for elevation or spiritual improvement. We could think that, at the present time, there is an emptying of symbolic and cultural production, the "great culture", to the detriment of "entertainment culture" or "mass culture"

(Arendt, 2000), and that Adorno (1968/2004) denounced as a "mutilation of the spirit".

References

Adorno, T. W. (1968/2004). *Lições de Sociologia* [Sociologie lessons]. Lisboa: Edit. 70.

Anzieu, D. (1979). Préface. In B. Grunberger & J. Chasseguet-Smirgel (Orgs.), *La Sublimation [Sublimation] – Les sentiers de la création* (pp. 11–23). Paris: Tchou, éditeur.

Arendt, H. (2000). A crise na cultura: Sua importância social e política [Crisis in culture: Its social and political importance]. In S. Lafer & J. S. Carvalho (Eds.), *Entre o Passado e o Futuro* (pp. 248–281). São Paulo: Editora Perspetivas.

Freud, S. (1905/1975). *Três Ensaios Sobre a Teoria da Sexualidade* [Three essays on theory of sexuality]. Lisboa: Livros do Brasil.

Freud, S. (1907/1981). El poeta y los sueños diurnos [Creative writers and daydreaming]. In *Sigmund Freud, Obras Completas* (Tomo II, pp. 1343–1348). Madrid: Biblioteca Nueva.

Freud, S. (1908/1982). La Moral Sexual "Cultural" y la Nerviosidad Moderna ["Cultural" Sexual Morality and Modern Nervous"]. In *Sigmund Freud, Obras Completas* (Tomo II, pp.1249–2033). Madrid: Biblioteca Nueva.

Freud, S. (1910/1981). Un Recuerdo Infantil de Leonardo de Vinci [Leonardo Da Vinci and a memory of his childhood]. In *Sigmund Freud, Obras Completas* (Tomo II, pp. 1579–1619). Madrid: Biblioteca Nueva.

Freud, S. (1911/1981). Los Dos Principios del Funcionamento Mental [Formulations on the two principles of mental functioning]. In *Sigmund Freud, Obras Completas* (pp. 1638–1642). Madrid: Biblioteca Nueva.

Freud, S. (1913/1981). Totem y Tabu [Totem and Taboo]. In *Sigmund Freud, Obras Completas* (Tomo II, pp. 1747–1850). Madrid: Biblioteca Nueva.

Freud, S. (1914/1981). Introduccion al narcisisme [On narcissisme: An introduction]. In *Sigmund Freud, Obras Completas* (Tomo II, pp. 2017–2033). Madrid: Biblioteca Nueva.

Freud, S. (1923/1981). El 'yo' y el 'ello' [The ego and the id]. In *Sigmund Freud, Obras Completas* (Tomo III, pp. 2701–2728). Madrid: Biblioteca Nueva.

Freud, S. (1927/1981). Dostoyewsky y el Parricidio [Dostoyewsky and the parricide]. In *Sigmund Freud, Obras Completas* (Tomo III, pp. 3004–3015). Madrid: Biblioteca Nueva.

Freud, S. (1929/1981). *El Malestar en la Cultura* [Civilization and its discontents]. In *Sigmund Freud, Obras Completas* (Tomo III, pp. 3017–3067). Madrid: Biblioteca Nueva.

Kris, E. (1952/1965). *Psychoanalytic exploration in art*. New York: International University Press.

Laplanche, J. & Pontalis, J.-B. (1967/1970). *Vocabulário da Psicanálise* [Vocabulary of psychoanalysis]. Lisboa: Morais.

Laplanche, J., & Pontalis, J.-B. (1975/1977). *Problématiques III: La Sublimation* [Issues III: Sublimation]. Paris: PUF.

Ortega y Gasset, J. (1946/1993). Las Dos Grandes Metáforas [The two great metaphors]. In *Ortega y Gasset, Obras Completas* (Tomo II, 2ª ed., pp. 332–401). Madrid: Alianza Edit.

Steinberg, L. (1972). *O Outro Critério* [The other criteria]. Rio-de-Janeiro: Cultura Brasil.

2 The need for repair as an impetus for artistic creation

The repair of the internal object

Kleinian psychoanalysis has provided countless contributions to the understanding of human creativity and the psycho-emotional goals of creative work, as well as to aesthetics and form in art, with perhaps the most precious contribution being the concept of reparation, which has enormous heuristic value when applied to the understanding and motivations of the creative act.

For Klein (1921/1968, 1927/1996, 1929/1996, 1930/1996, 1940/1996, 1946/1996), the creative impulse is contemporary with the depressive phase. It arises from the need to repair the lost object at the moment when it, in contrast to the previous schizo-paranoid phase, is experienced in its entirety and in its permanence, that is, when the good and bad aspects of the object are apprehended in a synthetic way. The recognition of the global character of the object confronts the subject with his own ambivalence, leading him to recognize the coexistence of good and bad in himself. This feeling of guilt arises from this process. Persecutory ideas do not disappear entirely, the subject continues to fear retaliation, on the part of the object, for his attacks. This fear, linked to guilt, leads him to try to fix, repair the object.

In *The Language of Psychoanalysis* (1967/1970), Laplanche and Pontalis give us the following definition of reparation:

> A mechanism, described by Melanie Klein, by which the individual seeks to repair the effects produced on his object of love by his destructive ghosts. This mechanism is linked to depressive distress and guilt: the phantasmatic repair of the maternal object, external and internal, would allow it to overcome the depressive position, guaranteeing the ego a stable identification with the beneficial object.
>
> (p. 581)

DOI: 10.4324/9781003329015-2

The repair cannot be seen as a simple defense mechanism against depressive anxiety. It is more of a modification and, as such, it should be understood, like sublimation, as a strategy for managing the impulses and not as a defense against them – an "acceptance mechanism" in Grotstein's terminology (1983). The repair experience is an experience of tolerance of loss and guilt, as well as responsibility for loss, while feeling that all is not lost. The possibility of mending, fixing, restoring, keeps hope alive. That is why Hinshelwood says that "repair is the strongest element of constructive and creative impulses" (1991/1992, p. 456). For Segal (1952/1982), the work of art represents an elaboration of the destructive drives and the guilt that is linked to them at the same time as it represents a triumph over the inner chaos of the creator. The artist acts under the influence of the childlike position and seeks to repair with his artistic activity a harmonious internal world that he feels he has possessed and fears to have lost due to his aggressiveness, but it is not enough to recreate anything in his internal world corresponding to the recreation of his own internal objects. The artist also tries to internalize the recreated object and communicate its own life in the external world.

In Marcel Proust

Among all artists, Proust (1871–1922) is the one who seems to give the most complete description of this creative process with *Recherche*, a monumental work with around a thousand pages and unfolding in seven volumes (written between 1913 and 1927). For him, it is the need to rediscover lost time, symbolically recreating it. But the exclusively intellectual recollection or memory, if it exists, is a dead recollection and devoid of any emotional value. A true memory, a bit of life appears, unexpectedly, sometimes in an occasional association: the taste of a cookie, the rattle of a carriage, for example, can revive fragments of intense emotion. As Fernandez (1992) reminds us, Proust rediscovers, throughout the various volumes of *Recherche*, his past, making all his lost, destroyed, loved objects parade: his parents, his grandmother, his dear Albertine, his cousins, etc. And thanks to his writing, to his art, he will be able to revive, in his work, his objects. For him, artistic creation essentially means fighting to recover time and lost objects. Hauser synthesizes this problem with great relevance:

> The struggle undertaken by the artist in relation to the past is, in fact, a struggle for what is real. The present is always "lost time", a loss of ourselves and those who belong to us; art, on the other hand, is a recreation in the sense of Proust, the only possible recreation of a world disintegrating around us and within us.
>
> (1958/1978, p. 131)

The repair of the self

We have seen that the repair of the object insofar as it derives from the feeling of guilt comes, at least in part, from the superego in its opposition to sadistic and destructive impulses. These impulses are then repressed and counter invested. In this perspective, the creative act and the reparative act appear closer to reactive formation than to sublimation.

This fact led Chasseguet-Smirgel to question why artistic creation often originates from feelings of guilt, in that it would be entirely in agreement with the superego, illustrating with clinical examples that show how artistic creation is often felt by the author as having been carried out at the expense of the object. To her, there are two types of creation in relation to reparation: one that enriches and satisfies the ego (and that can engender guilt) and another that, in fact, repairs the object:

> I want to show here precisely that the creative act can actually plunge its roots in the desire to repair the object, but also that there is a creative activity in which the objective pursued is the repair of the subject itself. The two categories of creative acts, far from being confused or entangled in each other, are in fact radically opposed. Only the creative act whose purpose is the repair of the self, implies the existence of pulsating discharges that give it the dignity of sublimation.
>
> (1984, p. 400)

For the author, the creative act aims to restore the subject's own integrity. And what does she mean by "integrity"? This is what Chasseguet-Smirgel concludes based on her clinical cases of psychoanalytic treatment and also on certain extra-analytical observations: there is a "common node for creators", and considers

> the creative act an attempt to achieve integrity, that is, to overcome castration at all levels [...] it is a matter of filling creation with all the failures of maturation, at all stages of development, to achieve narcissistic completeness as advocated by Grunberger, that is, referring not to a static narcissistic stage, but a dynamic narcissism crossing all stages of pulsational maturation and expressing itself in the unconscious through the phallic image [...] it is the reconstitution of a whole and phallic body.
>
> (op. cit., p. 102)

In Frida Kahlo

The life and work of this Mexican painter clearly illustrates the power of the depressive position that can lead to symbolization and repair of the self (bodily and psychic). At the age of 19, Frida Kahlo (1907–1954) was the victim of an accident on public transport, suffering perforation and injuries of the body (pelvis and legs), especially in the spine, that forced her, throughout her life, to undergo prolonged hospital stays, painful postoperative surgeries, and suffer from intense and constant pain. It is during these periods that she begins to paint to distract herself and combat boredom and pain, as her father, also linked to the arts, designed an installation on the bed that allowed her to paint while lying down. Her painting was described as a form of self-therapy, an antidote to suffering as her way of dealing with physical and emotional pain, as well as her way of maintaining control over her body and feelings, which she found devastating.

Figure 2.1 The Broken Column (F. Kahlo, 1944). Source: Frida Kahlo: Diego Rivera e Frida Kahlo © 2022, Banco de México Diego Rivera Frida Kahlo Museums Trust, Mexico, D.F. / SPA

The painting *The Broken Column* was painted shortly after another intervention on the spine. The operation left her decumbent in bed and enclosed in a metallic vest that helped to mitigate the strong and constant pain she felt. We see her standing in the middle of an arid and harsh landscape. Her torso is surrounded by metal straps covered with canvas that exerts pressure: they support her back, preventing her body from ending in collapse, which is announced in the center of her chest. The vertebral column was replaced by a completely fractured ionic column, about to collapse, whose capital supports Frida's face, which, despite being bathed in tears, does not reveal any expression of pain.

That was how she represented herself, firm and defiant, before the spectator. The nails that pierce her body are the constant donor symbol it supports. The largest ones, embedded in the column, mark the damage caused to her column in the 1925 accident; as for those on the left, they represent the emotional pain caused by abortion, the impossibility of becoming pregnant, the separation from her great and turbulent love, muralist Diego Rivera, the isolation. She writes: "To have hope, to ward off fear, the broken column, the long and terrible look, without being able to walk the long path, to move my life, made of steel" (Kahlo, cit. by Waberer, 1994/2003). When asked why she constantly portrayed herself in her paintings – and everything in Frida Kahlo is self-awareness – she replied that it was because she felt alone and because it was the best thing she knew to do to relieve herself and feel whole.

In Toulouse-Lautrec

Another pertinent illustration of the reparative and compensatory function of creative activity in the psycho-emotional balance of its author is the case of the French painter Toulouse-Lautrec (1864–1901). Descended from a noble family and with great ambition for sporting life, at the age of 14, he is the victim of a disability caused by the exacerbation of a congenital arthrosis which, aggravated by two falls with fractures to both legs, turns him into a complex crippled individual, modifying his future and desires. Only five feet tall, a deformed and grotesque figure, he dedicates himself to painting (Fermigier, 1963/1972). His creative activity, with his unconventional productions, above all the masterful drawings of the legs of the dancing girls of the Moulin Rouge, as well as of the horses and greyhounds, is clearly the liberating and repairing expression of his damaged self.

In James Joyce

We have seen that the notion of reparation is the foundation of the Kleinian notion of the creative function, and that the two categories of creative and reparative acts can be observed in different individuals but can even coexist in the same subject.

Take the case of the brilliant Irish writer, James Joyce. The death of his brother George, to whom he was closely linked, from typhoid fever at the age of 14, served to strengthen his belief in literary immortality. Through literature, "that great memory that is bigger and more generous than our own memory, no life, no moment of exaltation is ever lost" (Pindar, 2004/2006, p. 40), Joyce tried to compensate, to repair the lost object, George's wasted life, entrusting it to the great memory of literature, describing his death in *Stephen Hero* while posing him as a younger sister Isabel. Later, when the French translator of his greatest work, *Ulysses*, asked him for a kind of schematic and explanatory grid for the book, Joyce was not very collaborative:

> If I already delivered everything on a tray, I would lose my immortality. I inserted so many riddles and puzzles that university professors will be entertained for centuries to discuss what I wanted to say and that is the only way to ensure immortality.
>
> (op. cit., pp. 101–102)

Or as Joyce once said: "My request is that my reader dedicate his entire life to reading my work" (op. cit., p. 156).

The illustration of this creator highlights the simultaneity of the repairing function of the lost object, his brother George, and the need to repair the self-damaged by the suffering of forgetfulness and disappearance, through the search for symbolic immortality and the search for attention from another.

The beauty line in Cruzeiro Seixas

In a search for meaning for the work of Cruzeiro Seixas, the last dean of the Portuguese surrealists who recently died at the age of one hundred, we dialogued with it in the light of the concepts of Kleinian psychoanalysis that we explained earlier.

In this perspective, Seixas' drawing composed of parts of one or several bodies and fragmented objects makes us feel, at first, the destruction of the attack and the anxiety characteristic of the paranoid–schizoid position defined by Klein (1935/1996, 1940/1996, 1946/1996). But, in a second moment, the picture evokes in us the union, a harmony, a feeling of unity, products of repair, of restoration, involving us in a certain depressive tranquility. This happens, from our point of view, due to the presence of the calm tonality of the background and, above all, to the pacifying line that seems to cross the painting. This line, which we call the 'beauty line', seems to unite the fragment, repair the destroyed, giving a calm and reassuring consistency

Figure 2.2 Stories Without Beginning and Without End... (C. Seixas, 1959).
Source: Cruzeiro Seixas: © Cruzeiro Seixas, SPA 2022

to the painting. In all of Seixas' work, the line is reassuring. The figures are constituted by metamorphosed beings, pieces of body, humans, and animals, of fragmented objects (partial elements), but a line appears that unifies and harmonizes these partial objects, creating, that is, a harmonious totality and, to this extent, the fragmentation, the destruction, and the consecutive restoration lead us back to the Kleinian understanding of the reintegrating and repairing potential of the depressive position (Klein, 1958/1996).

References

Chasseguet-Smirgel, J. (1984). *Pour une Psychanalyse de l'Art et de la Créativité* [For a psychoanalysis of art and creativity]. Paris: P.B.T.
Fermigier, A. (1963/1972). *Toulouse-Lautrec.* Lisboa: Livros do Brasil.
Fernandez, D. (1992). *L'Arbre Jusqu'aux Racines* [Tree to roots]. Paris: Grasset.
Grotstein, J. (1983). The significance of Kleinian contributions to psychoanalysis: IV – Critiques of Klein. *International Journal of Psycho-Analysis and Psycho-Therapy, 9,* 511–535.

Hauser, A. (1958/1978). *Teorias da Arte* [Art theories]. Porto: Presença.

Hinshelwood, R. D. (1991/1992). Introdução [Introduction]. In R. D. Hinshelwood (Ed.), *Dicionário do Pensamento Kleiniano* (pp. 15–20). Porto Alegre: Artes Médicas.

Klein, M. (1921/1968). Le Développement d'un Enfant [Child development]. In *Essais de Psychanalyse* (pp. 29–89). Paris: Payot.

Klein, M. (1927/1996). Tendências Criminosas em Crianças Normais [Criminal tendencies in normal children]. In *Melanie Klein – Amor, Culpa e Reparação* (pp. 199–2013). Rio-de-Janeiro: Imago.

Klein, M. (1929/1996). Situações de Ansiedade Refletidas em uma Obra de Arte e no Impulso Criativo [Anxiety situations reflected in a work of art and creative impulse]. In *Melanie Klein – Amor Culpa e Reparação* (pp. 241–248). Rio-de-Janeiro: Imago.

Klein, M. (1930–1996). A Importância da Formação de Símbolos no Desenvolvimento do Ego [The importance of symbol formation in ego development]. In *Melanie Klein – Amor Culpa e Reparação* (pp. 251–264). Rio-de-Janeiro: Imago.

Klein, M. (1935–1996). Uma Contribuição à Psicogénese dos Estados Maníaco-Depressivos [A contribution to the genesis of depressive manic states]. In *Melanie Klein – Amor, Culpa e Reparação* (pp. 304–329). Rio-de-Janeiro: Imago.

Klein, M. (1940/1996). O Luto e as Suas Relações com os Estados Maníaco-Depressivos [Mourning and its relations with depressive manic states]. In *Melanie Klein – Amor Culpa e Reparação* (pp. 387–412). Rio-de-Janeiro: Imago.

Klein, M. (1946/1996). Notes sur Quelques Mécanismes Schizoides [Notes on some schizoid mechanisms]. In J. Riviere (Ed.), *Dévelopements de la Psychanalyse* (pp. 274–300). Paris: Presses Universitaires de France.

Klein, M. (1958/1996). On the development of mental functioning. *International Journal of Psycho-Analysis*, *39*(213), 84–90.

Laplanche, J., & Pontalis, J.-B. (1967/1970). *Vocabulário de Psicanálise* [Psychoanalysis vocabulary]. Lisboa: Morais.

Pindar, I. (2004/2006). *Joyce*. Lisboa: Asa.

Segal, H. (1952/1982). Uma Abordagem Psicanalítica da Estética [A psychoanalytic approach to aesthetics]. In J. Salomão (Ed.), *A Obra de Melanie Klein* (pp. 185–206). Rio-de-Janeiro: Imago Editora, Ltda.

Waberer, K. (1994/2003). *Frida Kahlo Masterpieces*. Munique: Schirmer Art Books.

3 Dialogue between D. Winnicott and S. Arietti concerning *I and the Village* (Chagall, 1911)

The Winnicottian theory of personal maturation rests essentially on human (intra and interpersonal) communication and the various senses of reality that constitute existence.

We assume that the mental maturation, that is, the interior and relational enrichment and expansion of the human being, implies the capacity for full, harmonious, useful, and creative use of the countless psycho-affective and relational potentialities of the individual in relation to himself and to the outside world; It is about achieving the functioning of the mind in a whole and united way.

In this chapter, I would like to focus on achieving the 'binocular vision' of the self and the world, simultaneously objective and subjective, as one of the manifestations of human creative maturity. From this point of view, psycho-emotional maturity would be the ability to keep areas of subjective objects (objects of the 'self') connected together with others in which there is a relationship with objectively perceived objects (objects of the 'not-self') or, using Alfredo Naffah Neto's terminology, *subjective reason*, that which governs the *affairs* of the heart, preferentially investing in the internal, subjective world, and *objective*, utilitarian reason, fundamentally investing in the events of the external world.

Donald Winnicott and Silvano Arietti tell us about this kind of functioning and capacity present in the healthy and creative human but using different concepts: through *potential space* (Winnicott, 1971) and *tertiary thought processes* (Arietti, 1976).

Let us begin with Arietti and his *princeps* concept, the tertiary processes of mental functioning. It is based on the two main mental levels at work advocated by Freud (1911): the primary process, consisting of a mode of functioning of the unconscious mental functions of the mind, prevailing in dream activity; it operates differently from the secondary process, which is the way the mind works when it is awake and uses common logic. In fact, in anticipation of Freud's concept of tertiary process, in *The Two Principles*

DOI: 10.4324/9781003329015-3

of Mental Functioning, he states: "Art can reconcile both principles by their peculiar path" (1911/1981, p. 1641). In Grotstein's (1981/2003) line of thinking, the thought in the primary process is associated with an idiosyncratic, autochthonous view of the personal world, with the secondary process being related to an objective and interpersonal view of the world.

In *Creativity: The Magic Synthesis*, Arietti states: "I have proposed the term tertiary processes to designate this special combination of mechanisms of primary and secondary processes" (1976, p. 12). The tertiary process would combine the worlds of mind and matter, psychic reality and external reality, and often the rational and the irrational, enriching and expanding the individual within. What Arietti argues here is that one of the fundamental factors in the one and whole mind that characterizes a healthy and creative adult lies in the ability to fuse dream and reality as well as the remarkable ease and freedom of transitioning or harmonizing these two aspects of mental functioning.

Barcelonian writer Enrique Vila-Matas, in one of his last novels, *Looking Like Dilan* (2012), addresses this issue by meditating playfully on reality and fiction, by stating that a fictionist does not have to compete with newspapers and the "show of the world". Instead, it is his task to make the boundaries between reality and fiction permeable, for "reality can afford itself the luxury of being unbelievable".

Are we not close to the Winnicottian concept of potential space that also goes beyond the internality–externality dichotomy? How can the healthy and creative individual, like the creatively playing child, achieve a creative fusion, and find the intersection between inner psychic reality and outer material reality?

The elaboration of Winnicott's (1971) main concept, *potential space*, was greatly stimulated by the reflection of his childhood clinical experience, as well as the fact that his wife was a ceramist, and her writings, in which she established a relationship between child play and adult concentration: "When I began to see [...] that this utilization that was done of me could, not only be a defensive regression, but also correspond to an essential recurring phase of a creative relationship with the world" (Milner, 1952/1987, p. 55).

Defined by Winnicott as

This intermediate area of experience, undisputed as to belonging to internal or external (shared) reality, constitutes most of the baby's experience. It will survive throughout most of the baby's life, in the internal way of living that characterizes the arts, religion, imaginary life and creative scientific work.

(1971/1975, p. 25)

Therefore, an intermediate space between the inner and outer worlds.

There is, in Winnicott's theory, much that depends on this "potential space between the subjective object and the objectively perceived object, between the extensions of the self and the not-self" (op. cit., p. 139): it is the union of different realities, implying different and irreconcilable modes of mental approach and management, unifying the mind, making the subject more whole and better suited to living a healthier, more creative, and useful life.

Being the symbol of all that can sustain the psyche in the absence of the object, the potential space – true producer of symbolic activity – creates the possibility, through culture, for the subject to sustain and perform creatively.

However, Winnicott also proposes a definition of creativity that goes beyond the narrow framework of recognized cultural creations and productions (creation with a capital C) to consider it as a particular attitude or relationship to itself and the outside world. This attitude or relationship would be:

> A creative mode of perception that gives the individual the feeling that life is worth living; What opposes such a mode of perception is a submissive condescending relation to external reality; the world and its elements are recognized, but only as what needs to be adjusted and adapted.
>
> (op. cit., p. 91)

Marc Chagall, a surrealist artist, is someone who is in close contact with his interiority and reflects in his works his inner world, his poetic space, and his inner freedom. In the approaches that surrealism made to psychoanalysis, André Breton sought to establish a link between internal reality and external reality, evoking a reality beyond reality, a *surreality* (Breton, 1924/1976). In a lecture on the nature of his painting, Chagall stated:

> The good old days are past, those when art fed exclusively on elements from the outside world, the world of shapes, lines and colors. Today, we are interested in everything, not only in the outer world, but also in the inner world of dreams and imagination.
>
> (Chagall cit. Baal-Teshuva, 1998/2008, p. 9)

Both the concept of surreality and this statement fit perfectly with the understanding of Winnicott's potential space and Arietti's tertiary process insofar as it defines itself as a transitive area between exterior and interior, objectivity and subjectivity, primary and secondary processes, emotion and reason, fantasy and reality, as a paradoxical space where inner and outer realities meet to create a new reality. In short, a space of 'magic synthesis' where contradictions are erased. The painter Mondrian has stated with remarkable clarity that the only problem with modern art is to strike a balance between the subjective and the objective.

The green portrait on the right side could very well be Chagall himself. A cow's-colored head looks closely into his eyes, while another cow is milked by a peasant inside his head. At the bottom are two other figures, one suspended and upside down. In this work, Chagall draws heavily on his Russian past (he has always remained true to his memories and feelings of love for Vitebsk, the village where he grew up).

This painting does not only represent the external, objective reality: the laws of anatomy, perspective, gravity, space and time, human–animal relations, these are not respected: all this is the translation of the primary process. But Vitebsk is perfectly recognizable: the manifestation of the secondary process. The transformation wrought by the painter allows us to recognize his world and discover new meanings. The village is not represented realistically, but psychologically. That is, it is represented in a condensation, a fusion (tertiary process) of realistic concepts and elements (secondary process) and feelings (primary process), such as joy, the love

Figure 3.1 I and the Village (Chagall, 1911). Source: Chagall: ©Marc Chagall, ADAGP 2022

for people, for nature, for animals, with their endless and ancient dialogue with humans. Reality and unreality are united, creating a surreality, a potential space where the irreconcilable contradictions between the subjective objects of the inner world (the 'I', the 'heart') and the objectively perceived objects (the 'not-self', the reality) are erased.

Chagall's revolution consists of reconciling the illustration of the world perceived by the senses, that is, the real, external, objective world, with the illustration of the presence of the poetic world of interiority, of subjectivity. It can be said that it is the psychologically illuminated outer world, pointing to a reality beyond the visible world. The present is not only the 'now', it is also the memory of the past and a projection into the future. This is why Chagall's art represents the painter's intimate autobiography. Could the 'art living' be part of the human being's ability to create and to activate that important area of experience located in the potential space between the subjective (Me-extensions) and their love objects (Non-Me) and to be able to enjoy it? This painting by Chagall is a symbol of this emotional life – the objective and subjective recreation of his dear Vitebsk, the Russian village to which he was always very attached internally despite being physically distant – which Freud stated, can only be known in terms of outer life.

Picasso once said: "When Chagall paints, it is not known whether he is sleeping at that moment or if he is awake. He must have, somewhere in his head, an angel". I would say that Chagall paints in a simultaneously dreamlike and vague mental register, synonymous with the vigorous action of potential space, this psychic 'place' that potentiates the blurring of distinctions that possibly exist only after Descartes' rationalism and allows the creative fusion of mental processes that, in a healthy and creative individual, should function in harmony and not separately. Our task in clinical work is to try to rescue this "angel" that allows the harmonization of autochthony and otherness or, to paraphrase Coimbra de Matos, to allow a full life that is "to live with our feet flat on the ground and with our heads in the moon, in order to be able to dream". Even the Romans said that the art of life is knowing how to harmonize *otium* with *negotium*.

References

Arietti, S. (1976). *Creativity: The magic synthesis.* New York: Basic Books, Inc. Publishers.

Breton, A. (1924/1976). Manifesto Surrealista [Surrealist manifesto]. In A. Breton (Ed.), *Manifesto do Surrealismo* (p. 58). Lisboa: Moraes.

Chagall, M. (1998/2008). *Chagall.* Koln: Taschen.

Freud, S. (1911/1981). Los dos principios del funcionamiento mental [The two principles of mental functioning]. In *Sigmund Freud. Obras Completas* (Tomo II, pp. 1638–1642). Madrid: Biblioteca Nueva.

Grotstein, J. (1981/2003). *Quem é o sonhador que sonha o sonho? Um estudo de presenças psíquicas* [Who is the dreamer who dreams the dream? A study of psychic presences]. Rio-de-Janeiro: Imago.

Milner, M. (1952/1987). Aspects of symbolism in comprehension of not-self. *International Journal of Psycho-Analysis*, *33*, 181–195.

Vila-Matas, E. (2012). *Ar de Dylan* [Looking like Dylan]. Lisboa: Teodolito.

Winnicott, D.W. (1971/1975). *Jeu et Réalité, l'Espace Potentiel* [Playing and reality]. Paris: Gallimard.

4 Wilfred Bion's concepts of continent function and SP<–>D in understanding artistic creative activity

Presentation of the concepts

To understand the role of the *continent function* in the artistic creative process, we will use Wilfred Bion's *Theory of Thought* (1962a/1991, 1962b/1979).

We will start this work by investigating the meaning and delimiting the definition of the concept. Although the continent function is not an explicit concept of metapsychology, this is where it delves into its roots. As Guillaumin (1987) reminds us with regard to this notion close to psychic work, this concept seems to be part of "the group of concepts, both descriptive and operative" that psychoanalysis uses in its clinical and also extra-clinical practice, in this case in understanding the creative activity. Its origins are diverse and go through simultaneous and different routes. However, Bion's influence (1963) was absolutely decisive, to the point of considering them as part of the fundamental elements in psychoanalysis.

In this way, we will investigate the relationship between the thinker/ creator and their thoughts according to the model of *intrapsychic projective identification* (activated creative thoughts) in the continent relationship (mind of the thinker). The *continent function* of the psyche is an active process (not limited to containing), which allows the mental contents (cognitive and emotional) to be tolerated and move within the creator's psychic apparatus in a state of unity and stability, protecting it from the feeling of instability or even psychic catastrophe (Bion, 1962b/1979). It is this *continent function* that allows for *creative flexibility* (Kubie, 1976), a condition of creativity, which signifies the flexible articulation of primary and secondary thought processes, joining the effort to associate, on the one hand, curiosity, innovation, fantasy and, on the other hand, organization, formalism, and the logical principle of non-contradiction.

This trajectory of the flight of scientific and poetic thought shows the importance of the *continent function* which, like a psychic skin, unifies,

DOI: 10.4324/9781003329015-4

gives coherence, acts as connecting force, and permits these various movements and cognitive operations, so disparate. In addition to creative flexibility, the *continent function* also allows for *negative capacity* (Bion 1963), another fundamental factor of creative personality, in that it not only allows us to account for all those elements and organize them but also, and above all, to open themselves to the unexplored of the internal and external world, to the doubt, the uncertainty, the mystery, and to tolerate it without disorganization. It also allows us to welcome emotions, anxieties, and needs within ourselves, decode them, detoxify them, understand them, so that they can be named and treated at a symbolic level.

The writer André Malraux stated that creation, especially artistic creation, "runs, as a rule, all the experiences of consciousness, from the sensory elements to the intellection and abstraction" (1974); a statement perfectly corroborated by the Bionian theory of thought (1962a) that thinking and creating is transforming. In fact, the psychological analysis of the creative experience reveals that the artist (and especially the modern artist), often turns to the depth of his inner reality (psychic and sensory), from where he rips the themes that serve as the basis of its creation. And, climbing one by one the pathways of his consciousness in various transformations of thought, he manages to achieve a universal message, rich in symbolism and meaning. This theory was deepened and expanded by Amaral Dias (1997, 2004), according to which the *alpha function* (transforming function) exists in all these passages of the various experiences of consciousness, which is the path of symbolization, the process of thinking, and the process of creation.

For Bion (1963), the creative effort, not only artistic but also scientific, is seen as a small-scale process of small oscillations between the fragments and the whole, of balancing between the paranoid–schizoid position and the depressive position of mental functioning, with this oscillatory process being represented by the symbol *SP<−>D*. It is these oscillations that we will address, both from a cognitive point of view and from an emotional point of view, taking into account that it is the continent function that enables creative experience, which assumes a continuous balance between disruptive thinking and organized thinking, between primary and secondary thought processes, between destructuring and integration.

From a cognitive point of view

It was Guilford who opened the modern era in research on creativity with his presidential speech at the American Psychological Association, in which he defined the notion of intelligence in such a way that creativity has a place of its own there: "Perhaps the most important thing in these investigations is the discovery that almost all men are creative, at least to a certain extent and in a certain way" (1950, p. 445). Especially useful in clarifying creativity and our purpose, was the distinction that the psychologist made between two types of thinking: *divergent thinking* that points to the type of responses that are neither known nor expected. "Divergent production: creation of information from the information given, in which there is persistence in the variety and quantity of production (out-put) from the same source. A shorter definition could be: the creation of logical alternatives" (Guilford, 1980, p. 454). *Convergent thinking* points to the known and the expected. "Convergent production: creation of information from the information given, in which there is persistence in achieving unique results or conventionally accepted as the best [...] A shorter definition could be: the creation of logical needs" (op. cit., p. 454). It is the balanced oscillation between these two types of thinking (dispersive and integrative), characteristic respectively of the cognitive aspect of the paranoid–schizoid and depressive positions, that produces cognitive flexibility, fundamental in the creative process.

From the point of view of mental and emotional processes

We know how Bion (1962a/1991, 1963) went further than Klein (1935/1996, 1946/1996) when, while studying the creative processes linked to knowledge, he disagreed that creativity was simply a progressive and unidirectional movement of the schizo-paranoid position (SP) to the depressive position (D), the latter being the one that would enable a capacity for synthesis and reformulation of a new set of ideas, values, and positions. For Bion, instead of a progressive and unidirectional movement, the creative process consists of an alternative oscillatory movement, between the paranoid–schizoid position (SP) and the depressive position (D). Bion described the type of unconscious activity present in this process: the loosening of all ties that connect the known stabilized elements, with a later reformulation around a new focal point, the selected fact. The loosening of the integration represents the characteristic activity of the paranoid–schizoid position and the reformulation represents the fundamental activity of the depressive position. There is thus a continuous movement of back and forth between the two positions, allowing one to evaluate the modification of the subject's anxieties, mental mechanisms, and type of object relationships.

Application of Bionian concepts to creative work

We will use the models of the relationship between *continent/content* (mind/ thoughts) and PS<–>D to the creative dynamics of artistic activities:

Any creator who starts the adventure of exploring a new theme, for example, the writer who starts a novel, or the scientist who starts a new investigation, is faced, in a first phase, with feelings of chaos and fragmentation (schizoid and paranoid anxieties). In a second phase of the creative process, the subject prepares a "receptive uterus" (Ehrenzweig, 1967/1974) to retain and integrate the fragmented and dispersed material. If integration has been successful, schizoid anxieties will give way to depressive anxieties. In the third phase, the creator will be able to re-project the work at a higher level, symbolized through the word. These transformations are repeated throughout the creative process until the conclusion of the work.

In Picasso's cubism

Pablo Picasso (1881–1973) is the painter who, in our eyes, best embodies the spirit of modern art, with the cubist style where the models of perception and representation used are highly revolutionary and contradictory. Since the development of cubism, two principles of representation have coexisted in Picasso's work. We can designate them by the terms of dissociation and figuration, defined by Carsten et al. in their admirable work on the work of the Spanish painter:

> The term "figuration" refers to art that reproduces nature in an imitative way, the term "dissociation" designates, on the other hand, art as an autonomous manifestation, which moves away from the natural model without trying to reproduce it. These two artistic forms alternate and interpenetrate in all of Picasso's work.
>
> (2002, p. 403)

Paul Klee (1961), painter and painting theorist, would say that in Picasso's cubism there are two "looks", a "gaze", figurative, imitative (mimesis), which reproduces nature, representing the objective point of view; and the "mobile gaze", dispersive, dissociative, in which the painter's subjectivity is sought, in detriment of the reproduction of the object – not forgetting the statement of the painter Braque: "Reality only manifests itself when it is illuminated by the light of poetry" – and reveals the existence of an emotional relationship in each of the details of that extract.

This mode of figurative representation, associated with figurative representation and dissociative representation, which alternate and oscillate constantly, represents 'synthetic cubism', the greatest expression of cubism, and we think we can equate, on the mental plane, the mental processes characteristic of the depressive and paranoid–schizoid positions and their constant oscillation. This process seems to represent the creative effort as Bion (1963) conceived it, that is, as a small-scale process of movements back and forth between the two mental positions (SP<–>D).

This painting, composed of a mixture of complex images, has a certain characteristic that is more 'real' than a simple photograph or a realistic painting of the object in question, the violin. The mixture of images simultaneously sends to the different aspects of the object (realistically and subjectively – like the strings that evoke sound vibration) and visual perspectives of the observer (from the side, from the front). And, despite a mixture of displaced forms, the painting does not evoke any disorder or chaos.

This picture represents his lover's face. A profile starts to stand out in the contoured form (depressive position, figuration, integration, stare), but immediately the rounded, loving elements of a counter-natural front view are noticed (paranoid–schizoid position, dissociation, mobile look). But this unnatural coexistence exists in a representation of a figure characterized by an exact balance in the combination of methods of dissociative and figurative representation – the painter preserves principles of psychotic creations that are unknown: the perspective and balance of the composition.

In fact, cubist fragmentation is dangerously close to psychotic art. But, while the fractures of psychotic art remain isolated, the cubist fragmentation

375. PICASSO : *Violon et raisins*. 1912. New York, The Museum of Modern Art.

Figure 4.1 Violin and Grapes (Picasso, 1912). Source: Picasso: ©2022, Succession Pablo Picasso, SPA

Figure 4.2 Portrait of Marie-Thérèse Walter (Picasso, 1937). Source: Picasso: ©2022, Succession Pablo Picasso, SPA

is resolved by an in-depth coherence that belongs to a deeper level of psychic experience. If there is dissociation, it is only superficial and conscious, because on the deep plane there is integration. On the criticisms of Picasso's works, in which there seems to be a lack of unity, indicating his mental insanity, Pichon Rivière wrote:

> It is not so. An in-depth analysis will show that the artist saw the work as a path of investigation, he went down to the most regressive stages of the unconscious itself. But he didn't get lost, he didn't go crazy, he didn't die. There, he found the root of his vital and communicative unity – as in Guernica.
>
> (Pichon-Rivière, 1987)

He did not succumb to the enormous pressure of his own unconscious as the psychotic artist succumbs. This is the power of the continent function for the psyche.

In the polyphonic musical field

In the field of polyphonic music defined by Faria as "the art of simultaneous melodies" (1973, p. 411), characterized by a process of musical composition combining several melodies that develop independently, but within the same tone, we call attention to the particularity of polyphonic hearing, in which the attentive auditor lets his attention oscillate freely between the focused (integrative) and non-focused (dispersive) states. Now it focuses on the consistent sounds of the chords, now it drains your attention so that you can fully embrace the softer and more transparent weave of the polyphonic voices. It progressively moves from one level to another, with a continuous oscillation between these two types of attention and auditory enjoyment (Guerling, 2009).

From a psychoanalytic perspective, we can bring the discourse on tonal and atonal music back to the opposite effect that these different forms can have on the impact with our internal world: tonal music, being able to promote a process of psychic integration that, with the resolution of dissonances, would facilitate the organization, restoration, and reconstruction of internal objects (an operation that is linked to the depressive position), while atonal music, with the dissonances that it implies, would facilitate the separation, fragmentation, and disorganization of the same objects (modalities that characterize the paranoid–schizoid position).

In psychoanalysis: a floating attention

Defined by Laplanche and Pontalis in his *Psychoanalysis Vocabulary* as follows:

> The way in which, according to Freud, the analyst must listen to the analysand: he must not privilege a priori any element of his discourse, which implies that he lets function as freely as possible their own unconscious activity and suspend the motivations that usually direct their attention.
>
> (1967/1970, p. 74)

It is a type of oscillating attention, between dispersion and integration, between convergence and divergence, between the interior (feelings and thoughts of the psychoanalyst) and the exterior (patient).

The technique of floating attention in psychoanalysis is very similar to polyphonic hearing in atonal music and the multidimensional vision of painters (Klee, 1961) in that it implies oscillatory demands between opposite positions.

In modern dance (contract <–> release)

The aim of modern dance is to transmit to the public a sense of the interior and exterior reality. Martha Graham (1894–1991) was, in the 1920s and 1930s, one of the pioneers of modern dance, creating a style that sought to give more emphasis to the senses and dreams, trying to theatrically maximize them through body movements (Fahllbush, 1990). Indeed, interested in Freudian theories and searching the depths of the soul for the movement of the spirit to plunge into the unknown of being, she is one of the choreographers who best reveals the pulse of the psyche. The technical principle of the *contract/release* makes the torso follow the deepest emotions of the psyche; considering the statement that movement is born from the body itself, it can be said that Martha Graham relocated the psyche from the brain to the spine and the solar plexus, these being the thinking elements. Here are some fundamentals of her school: the solar plexus is considered a source of energy for movement; the torso concentrates the vital forces that radiate to the limbs; the pelvic region is a point of support and representative of sexuality – the strength of the gesture happens in the function of the strength of the emotion (Bourcier, 1987).

For another great modern dance choreographer, Pina Bausch (1943–2011), the body, that knot of languages, is the great translator of emotions and thoughts of different states of mind, different cultures, identities, different expressions of being (Servos, 1998). It is through the body in action in dance that we move from physiology to psychology, from anatomy to aesthetics, from physics to metaphysics, from sensation to representation. To translate, this is what the bodies do in these theater dances. The sense of movement means thinking about what it means to propose a certain image, gesture, or rhythm, in relation to the resonance it has with the interior life or with the reality that is greater than that of the stage, with which it must be related (Roquet, 1991).

Dance is the rhythmic–gestural expression of human feelings. This statement is even more pertinent in modern and contemporary dance, where the different emotional states are supposed to be clearly expressed by the movements of the body.

Analyzing the sequence of these movements/theatricalizations, we can identify and follow the sequence of emotional states, using the Bionian concept of oscillations between the paranoid–schizoid and depressive positions (SP<–>D) (Bion, 1963).

As we have already seen, this is the mathematical notation created by Bion to represent the free movement that the human mind can make between the two positions described by Klein. Here are some of its manifestations:

the first provokes feelings of omnipotence, omniscience, persecution, annihilation, a sense of fragmentation, an inability to hold a global and realistic perception of the internal and external world; the second mental position enables experiences of hatred and love that can be associated, the need for reparation and the relationship with the total object, as well as more realistic perceptions of personal abilities and limitations, ultimately, of human fallibility and finitude.

Vaclav Havel (1936–2011), statesman and man of culture and art, once stated that it is the first time in human history that an "atheist civilization" has been experienced, in which man considers himself "omnipotent and omniscient", without any "humility". Alongside this characteristic of contemporaneity, we have fragmentation, which is certainly also one of its greatest characteristics. Couldn't the convulsive, tense, short, sometimes paroxysmal movements of contemporary dance be associated with the paranoid–schizoid mental position (SP)? In turn, the unity, a greater constancy and regularity, characteristic of other times and other forms and rhythms of life, translated into dance by broader, paused, dilated, and stretched movements, can it not translate the depressive position (D)?

In this way, is the oscillation of the body language "contract/release" initiated by Martha Graham in modern dance not equivalent to the SP <–> D of Wilfred Bion's mental language?

To create is to transform: the genesis of a poem by Aldous Huxley

Transcription of four versions of a Huxley verse (1970, p. 37):

1st – "Evoking the flash moment"
2nd – "Evoking the frightened flash of momentary eyes and wings that pass by"
3rd – "Calling to life the flash of the momentary wing and the frightened eye"
4th – "Evoking the scared wing and the momentary eye out of nowhere"

Huxley's project was to poetically write an experience that startled him: one night, when he was driving his car on a country road, he came across the sudden vision of animal eyes on the road. In this vulgar experience of surprise, the poet discovers an interesting aspect: at night, an ephemeral glow denounces the presence of eyes that stalk us in the darkness. The tranquility of the landscape is altered by that anonymous look that, for an instant, introduces a threatening mirage into our lives.

The genesis of this poem is not only about stylistic purification. It is also a dynamic that goes from the vague to the concrete, from the sensory not thought to the psychic thought, in short, an increase in the level of thought. We are immediately led to think of the vertical axis of the

Bionian Grid (Bion, 1964/1977) that accounts for the various stages of the development of thoughts through the *alpha function*, this "abstraction designating the device capable of transforming the sensory impressions of emotional experiences into thoughts increasingly abstract" (op. cit., p. 19), that is, the transformation from the sensory elements, not psychically processed (the *beta elements*, in this case, the physical sensation of fear) to the highly stylized concepts (the poem's final form). Let us remember Malraux (1974) again: "Creation, as a rule, goes through all the experiences of consciousness, from the sensory elements to the intellection and abstraction".

References

Amaral Dias, C. (1997). *Tabela para uma Nebulosa* [Grid for a nebula]. Lisboa: Fim de Século.
Amaral Dias, C. (2004). *Costurando as Linhas da Psicopatologia Borderland* [Sewing the lines of borderland psychopatology]. Lisboa: Climepsi.
Bion, W. (1962a/1991). Uma teoria do pensar [A theory of thinking]. In E. B. Spillius (Ed.), *Melanie Klein Hoje* (Vol. 1, pp. 185–193). Rio-de-Janeiro: Imago.
Bion, W. R. (1962b/1979). *Aux Sources de l'Expérience* [Learning from experience]. Paris: PUF.
Bion, W. R. (1963). *The elements of psycho-analysis*. London: Eineman.
Bion, W. R. (1964/1977). *A grade*. [Two papers: The grid and the caesura]. Rio-de-Janeiro: Imago.
Bourcier, P. (1987). *História da Dança no Ocidente* [History of the dance in occident]. São Paulo: Martins Fontes.
Carsten, S., Warncke, P., Walter, I. F., & Warncke, I. F. (2002). *Picasso*. Koln: Tashen.
Erhrenzweig, A. (1967/1974). *L'Ordre Caché de l'Art* [The hidden order of art]. Paris: Gallimard.
Fahlbush, H. (1990). *Dansa Moderna-Contemporânea* [Modern-contemporary danse]. Rio-de-Janeiro: Luiza Gomes.
Faria, M. (1973). Polifonia [Polyphony]. *Enciclopédia Luso Brasileira da Cultura* (Tomo 15, pp. 411–419). Lisboa: Verbo.
Guerling, C. C. (2009). *Uma Introdução às Teorias Analíticas da Música Atonal* [An introduction to atonal music theories]. Rio-de-Janeiro: ANPPOM.
Guilford, J. P. (1950). *Traits of creativity*. New York: Penguin.
Guilford, J. P. (1980). Teorias de la Inteligencia [Inteligence theories]. In J. G. Sevilla (Ed.), *Manual de Psicologia General* (Edited by Martinez Rocos, Vol. III, pp. 440–470). Barcelona: Martinez Rocos.
Guillaumin, J. (1987). La Création Artistique et l'Elaboration Consciente de l'Inconscient, Avec des Considérations Particulières Sur la Création Poétique [Artistic creation and the conscious elaboration of the unconscious, with particular considerations about poetic creation]. In D. Anzieu, M. Mathieu,

36   *Bion's concepts of continent function*

M. Besdine, E. Jacques, & J. Guillaumin (Eds.), *Psychanalyse du Génie Créateur* (pp. 265–280). Paris: Dunod.

Huxley, A. (1970). *Aldous Huxley, Poesia* [Aldous Huxley, poetry]. Barcelona: Edt. Univ. Almeria.

Klee, P. (1961). *The thinking eye*. London: Lund Humphries.

Klein, M. (1935/1996). Uma Contribuição à Psicogénese dos Estados Maníaco-Depressivos [A contribution to the psycho-genesis of manic-depressive states]. In *Melanie Klein – Amor, Culpa e Reparação* (pp. 304–329). Rio-de-Janeiro: Imago.

Klein, M. (1946/1983). Notes Sur Quelques Mécanismes Schizoides [Notes on some schizoid mechanisms]. In *Développements de la Psychanalyse* (pp. 274–300). Paris: PUF.

Kubie, L. S. (1976). Creation and neurosis. In A. Rothenberg & C. R. Hausman (Eds.), *The creativity question* (pp. 143–148). Durham, NC: Duke University Press.

Laplanche, J. & Pontalis, J.-B. (1967/1970). *Vocabulário da Psicanálise* [Vocabulary of Psychoanalysis]. Lisboa: Morais.

Malraux, A. (1974). *Psychologie de l'Art: La Monnaie de l'Absolu*. Paris: Gallimard.

Pichon-Rivière, E. (1987). *El Proceso Creador* [The creative process]. Buenos Aires: Nueva Visión.

Roquet, C. (1991). *Vu du Geste: Interpeler le Mouvement Dansé* [Gesture vue: To challenged danced movement]. Paris: CND.

Servos, N. (1998). *Pina Bausch: Danse Theater*. Munich: K. Kieser Uerlag.

5   Bion and the popes of horror

Theory of transformations

Diego Velázquez's painting, *Pope Innocent X* (1650), can be found in Rome, in the Doria Pamphili Gallery. It is a realistic painting depicting a pope who is brilliant, radiant, magnificent, and secure. In short, a pope symbolizing the robustness of one of the fundamental pillars of Western culture and civilization. When the Pope saw Velázquez's painting for the first time, he exclaimed "Troppo vero!". Three hundred years later, Francis Bacon saw a reproduction of the painting and assembled a vast collection of reproductions, through which he came to study and know the painting deeply. Between 1951 and 1965, Bacon painted 45 studies, variations, reactions to Velázquez's painting, always feeling a strong obsession for it.

Before we go on to describe Bacon's first study of the painting, I propose that we first listen to the painter himself about the meaning and technique of his painting in general, as well as the historical and cultural circumstances of the time:

> Art is a method of opening up areas of sensitivity, rather than the mere illustration of an object.
>
> (Bacon cited by Sinclair, 1995, p. 232)

> I paint forces, not figures.
>
> (interview with Sylvester, 2007)

> A big part of a painting is always a convention, the appearance, and that's what I try to eliminate from my paintings. I look for the essential, that the painting takes on, in the most direct way possible, the material identity of what it is I'm representing. My way of distorting images brings me far closer to human beings than if I just sat down and did their portrait [...] I tried to find a technique capable of reproducing the profound reality and not the appearance of people.
>
> (interview with Ramón Chao, 1982)

DOI: 10.4324/9781003329015-5

Figure 5.1 Pope Innocent X (Velázquez, 1650). Source: Francis Bacon: © Estate of Francis Bacon/DACS 2022

In short, what Bacon attempts to capture is the emotional and sensitive state of a subject in any given moment – his objective is to capture an identity.

Like many other post-World War II artists, he tried to reproduce the climate of absolute terror and disbelief in the culture, expressing what happened to humanity after the War and the Nazi Holocaust. Bacon never paints the figuration of horror, there is never any narration or illustration of a horror scene. What he paints is the scream as a capture of an invisible force. His objective is to express the torturous reality of the contemporary man, traumatized by the impossibility to eradicate Evil, worse yet, by the complete disbelief in civilizational and cultural progress, by the maddening paradox of the association between progress and barbarism. What Bacon intends to metaphorize is the afflictive and rabid helplessness of the disaster in culture, the disenchantment of the world. I remember the lucid words of Primo Levi in, and the title is accurate, *If This Is A Man*: "The offense made to the human being […] the insurmountable nature of the offense that spreads like a disease, which is an inexhaustible source of evil" (*The Truce*, 1963/2010, p. 9). What Bacon lets us see is a metaphor of the internal feeling towards the total bankruptcy of culture, as Freud conceived in the

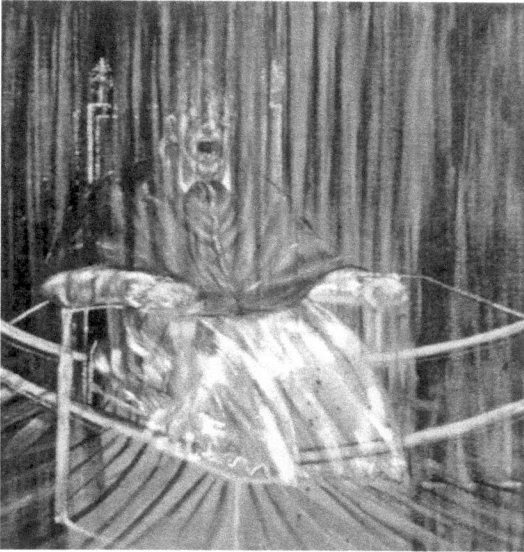

Figure 5.2 The Screaming Pope (Bacon, 1953). Source: Francis Bacon: © Estate of Francis Bacon/DACS 2022

beginning of his essay, *The Future of an Illusion* (1927/1981). Why choose the figure of the pope? Precisely because he represents one of the major foundations of our Western civilization.

Francis Bacon's painting, *Study After Velázquez's Portrait of Pope Innocent X* (1953), better known as *The Screaming Pope*, presents us with a vociferous and desperate papal figure in free fall, enclosed in a chair and a cube, with his upper body blurred between the curtains in the background and a tassel on top of the place that should be occupied by the brain. Beyond the feeling of a downward movement of the figure, when Bacon paints the pope who screams, there is nothing that provokes horror, and the curtain before him is not only a way to isolate him – to subtract him from view – it is also to show that he sees nothing, he screams before the invisible.

In addition to the fierce criticism of 'organized religion' in the form of screams and sneers of a king of the Catholic Church and monarch of the world, Bacon put his deepest fears and angers on the canvas, expelled them, and attained a new intensity. Let us not forget that Bacon brings with him a childhood marked by death (of two sisters), a youth disturbed by the extreme incomprehension of his father (he expelled him from home for his homosexual manifestations), the suicide of two of his lovers, as of all the horror of Ireland's civil war, both World Wars, and the beginning of the Cold War. The figure vertiginously falling and screaming, solitary and caged, without any possibility of escape, is an endless mask of suffering, anger, anguish, of helplessness and terror, of decrepitude and death.

Despite all the realism of his painting, Bacon believed that there were "inner realities", even admitting that Freud's works had modified his own sense of realism, "because we became more aware of how realism can be fed by the subconscious. [...] We live almost all the time covered by veils ... It is a veiled existence". Indeed, Bacon's picture is a lifting of the veil of the appearances of Velázquez's representation, confronting himself and the spectator with "the brutality of the facts", with the spasmodic and convulsive cry, in order to directly and violently hit the nervous system. First sit down and then think. According to Paul Klee's famous formula, "instead of giving the visible, make it visible", in art it is not a matter of reproducing or inventing forms, but of grasping forces (Klee, cited by Deleuze, 1984). Bacon told a journalist that his studies of Velázquez were "an intention to turn a certain type of sensation into something visible".

Wilfred Bion states in his book *Transformations* (1965/1982), now a classic:

> The theory of transformations and its development do not belong to the central corpus of psychoanalytic theory, but to the practice of psychoanalytic observation. Psychoanalytic theories, as well as the statements of the patient or the analyst, are representations of an emotional experience. Understanding the process of representation will help us to understand representation and what is represented.
>
> (pp. 43–44)

The painter, through his artistic talent, managed to transform a person, a landscape ("the realization") into a painting ("representation"), thanks to the invariants. "I will call 'invariant' the elements that account for the unchanged aspect of transformation" (p. 7). And, further on:

> The analysis, in its pre-catastrophic state, is distinguished from the post-catastrophic state by the following characteristics: it is not emotional, theoretical, and devoid of any noticeable exterior modification ... In the post-catastrophic state, on the contrary, violence is obvious, but its ideological content, hitherto evident, seems to be lacking. The emotion is evident and reaches the analyst.
>
> (p. 15)

In our case it reaches the viewer. Bion proposes that the psychic transformations are processed by three different modalities, that he denominates "transformations of rigid movement", "projective transformations", and "transformations in hallucinosis".

In the present study, and according to Bion's theory, we conceive Velázquez's painting as a representation of Bacon's pre-catastrophic (the mind's neurotic part) state performing a rigid motion transformation, in which it minimally distorts the original fact – *Innocent X* – and allows the viewer to find the invariant element very easily ("Troppo vero!"). The apparent characteristics of the pope are visible: power, serenity, infallibility, protection, trust in the life of the beyond, belief in love.

The Screaming Pope, however, represents the projection of the mind in a post-catastrophic state, in a projective-type transformation, distorting the original fact more intensely due to intense emotions, distorting the notions of space/time and papal posture without, however, completely preventing the viewer from recognizing the invariants that make recognition possible.

In another study of *Pope Innocent X*, titled *Figure with Meat* (1954), we see, in lugubrious hues, a body that vanishes and decomposes, escaping through a screaming mouth, behind which two huge carcasses of animals appear hanging. Here we no longer distinguish the man from the animal,

Figure 5.3 Figure with Meat (Bacon, 1954). Source: Francis Bacon: © Estate of Francis Bacon/DACS 2022

the dead from the living. This totally disfigured and mutilated body, at the border of disappearance and confused with the flesh, suggests the loss of basic identity and the presence of death. "I am always aware of my mortal condition. And I hate this condition: I never want to die". Bacon feels touched by the smell of death and by the violence of life, in which "each one lives to eat the other" (Bacon cited by Sinclair, 1993/1995, p. 47). Bacon exposes in his work something of death and real incompleteness when he states: "There is always a sense of death in people when they see my paintings ... I may carry this feeling of death all the time ... I always surprise myself when I wake up in the morning" (op. cit., p. 78). In this artwork, the distortion is of such magnitude that it borders on the transformation into hallucinosis, related to a primitive catastrophe due to an anxiety of primordial annihilation, the subject finding no internal continent capacity, reintroduced in the form of an 'unnamed terror'. This canvas is clearly the representation of a catastrophic emotional experience: terror and pain in its pure state.

References

Bion, W. R. (1965/1982). *Transformations [Transformations]* – *Passage de l'Apprentissage à la Croissance*. Paris: PUF.

Chao, R. (1982). *Francis Bacon: o homem e o artista* [Francis Bacon: the artist and the man]. Revista E, 1991, 21–25.

Deleuze, G. (1984). *Francis Bacon, Logique de la Sensation* [Francis Bacon sensation logic]. Paris: Édition de la Différence.

Freud, S. (1927/1981). O Futuro de uma Ilusão [The future of an illusion]. In *Sigmund Freud, Obras Completas* (Tomo III, pp. 2962–2992). Madrid: Biblioteca Nueva.

Levi, P. (1963/2010). *A Trégua* [The truce]. Lisboa: Teorema.

Sinclair, A. (1995). *Francis Bacon. Una Vida en una Época de Violência* [Francis Bacon. A life in violent times]. Barcelona: S.A.

Sylvester, E. (2007). *Entrevistas com Francis Bacon* [Interviews with Francis Bacon]. Lisboa: Almedina.

6   Monologues and dialogues in James Joyce's work

Through the eyes of Bion and Ferro

We find ourselves fully in the relationship between literature and psychoanalysis. Not in the classical, Freudian psychoanalytic relationship, in which one sought to unravel the libidinal origin of aesthetic productions. For example, behind Da Vinci's *Mona Lisa*'s smile, Freud sees the traces of the original ghosts attached to the phallic mother (regarding their androgenic appearance) or in *The Brothers Karamazov*, the psychoanalyst finds the major motives of the Oedipal conflict in Dostoevsky's relationship with his father.

We focus on the thought processes mobilized in literary creation which, being an entirely mental, psychic activity, forces the author, when creating the text of fiction, to explore the rational and emotional functions in contact with the imaginary, that is, with psychic objects that are processed on an unconscious level and that take shape in the psychological personification of the characters. In fictional creation, both conscious and unconscious discourse, each with its own cognitive and temporal characteristics, enter/ inside the construction of stories and characters.

Two quotes from David Lodge, English novelist and essayist, from his book *Consciousness and the Novel* (2002/2009) in which he defines literature as "*the richest and most comprehensive record* [of human consciousness] *we have*" (p. 25, emphasis added) and "*as we enter the modern age, the emphasis increasingly falls on building a reality within the consciousness of the individual, the difficulty of representing these two distinct mental worlds, the distortion of consciousness by the unconscious, and the limits of human understanding*" (p. 56, emphasis added).

In this chapter we highlight the characteristics of James Joyce's creative dynamics, characterized by temporal and discursive cuts, and his peculiar way of thinking, by applying the Bionian model of the oscillation between the schizo-paranoid position (SP) and the depressive position (D), formulated by Bion as SP<–>D, in *Elements of Psychoanalysis* (1963).

DOI: 10.4324/9781003329015-6

Bion (1963) has taken from Klein (1946/1996) the importance of alternating between those positions (SP<->D) as central to mental life (and also to the creative process) and represents the basic mechanism of thought. He described the movement from a formless state of chaos to a state of coherence, which suddenly develops through the operation of a selected fact. Thus, from a purely cognitive point of view, in the schizo-paranoid position, the emphasis is placed on chaotic, dispersive thinking, while in the depressive position, the emphasis is on the primacy of integrative, coherent, socialized thinking.

James Joyce, an Irish novelist, short story writer and expat poet, widely regarded as one of the most prominent writers of the twentieth century, as he made a major contribution to the development of modernist literature, used the 'stream of consciousness' or 'current of consciousness' – a concept coined by the American psychologist William James and whose brother, novelist Henry James, was one of the greatest exponents – as a narrative technique, which became known as 'inner monologue', when the character's thoughts are continually presented, illogical, primary, unlike soliloquy, when a character orally and logically exposes his or her reflections (such as Shakespeare's characters). The use of this technique reveals the concern to work, in the literary piece, the issue of interiority, self-awareness, the present, allowing us to enter directly into the most intimate layers of the characters' minds. The richness of Joyce's novels is that it exposes the flow of the mind so that thoughts emerge spontaneously in the speech of the characters. For example, there are situations where Leopold Bloom (*Ulysses*), while waiting to be seen at the pharmacy, describes what is going on in his mind. This direct relationship with thoughts articulates the narrative with the immediate action of the character and allows the reader to come into contact with his or her interiority and present moment. The characters never fail to mentally, deeply, and thoroughly discuss the most mundane events. All the emphasis is placed on the reflection of events in the intimate mind of the characters – hence the extreme psychological density of the work.

The flow of consciousness or inner monologue or stream of thought can be understood psychoanalytically through Bion's inspired *reverie* model, which considers it to be the result of the ever-active alpha function of sensory turbulence and 'storms' in alpha elements, which will constitute "waking dream thinking" (Bion, 1962) and which Antonino Ferro designates as "transformations into dreams" (Ferro, 2017, p. 30) and which, using Bion's Grid (1962), shows that Joyce's psychic work lies within the grid line C (myths, dream thoughts, alpha sequences). Recalling Freud's wise maxim, "the gold of psychoanalysis is free association", necessary for analytic work, which happens just as the patient lowers the control of consciousness, letting the speech flow, thus revealing the dynamic relationships between conscious and unconscious processes of thought, we could say that the fundamental characteristic of Joyce's writing coincides perfectly with Antonino Ferro's fundamental rule of psychoanalysis: "the fundamental rule could be to dream sensorially so as to be more and more in touch with the unconscious" (2017, p. 40) "and experiencing it growing, session after session" (p. 30) – here we would say page after page.

Joyce's main novels' plot overview: *A Portrait of the Artist as a Young Man* is an autobiographical novel showing the achievement of maturity, self-awareness, and intellectual growth of an intelligent young man, Stephen Dedalus, a Joycean representation of himself, relating the process of his break with the Catholic Church and his disdain for Dublin's cultural and social provincialism. In *Ulysses* the action takes place on a single day, June 16, 1904, in Dublin. In a kind of rereading, a parody of Homer's *Odyssey*'s plot, in which Joyce creates an epic of modern times with not heroic, but average protagonists, with not exceptional, but mundane events, is the story of the antihero, Leopold Bloom (Ulysses), who wanders the streets of Dublin tormented by the suspicion that his wife, Molly Bloom, cheats on him (an unfaithful Penelope) but without the courage to take action, and the meeting with his son, Stephen Dedalus (Telemachus). It is thus a routine, ordinary day where ideas, thoughts, anguishes, and doubts parade in a ghostly way, described in as much detail as possible. If this novel is a day on the town, *Finnegans Wake* is a night and exclusively shares the logic of dreams, making the book virtually unreadable and without a specific plot.

The Bionian look at the process of creative elaboration of these novels clearly shows a constant balance between the disruptive, dispersive, dissociative, divergent, primary, dreamlike, proper position of the schizo-paranoid position and coherent, rational, logical, integrative, secondary, socialized thinking, characteristic of the depressive position. These fluctuations occur throughout much of Joyce's work and can be observed in filigree in each of his novels.

> When there is a narrative movement towards the coherence, stability and comprehensibility of the story, we are facing the dominance of the depressive position (dialogues). If, on the contrary, the story "deteriorates" in its comprehensibility or does not find sufficient stability in the developed theme, there is a reversal towards the cognitive functioning characteristic of the schizoparanoid position.
>
> (Delgado, 2011)

In his main novels – *A Portrait of the Artist and a Young Man* (1916), *Ulysses* (1922), and *Finnegans Wake* (1939), the reader follows two overlapping narrative plans: on the one hand the 'thought flow' of the main characters, on the other hand, the dialogue between the characters. The 'inner monologues', which occupy most of the novels, as Joyce gave much more importance to inner psychic reality than to outer reality, refer to the incessant whirl of thoughts in the conscious mind, that is, the whole range of impressions, sensations, fantasies, and reasonings that ceaselessly pass through the mind of the subject. In this intimate narrative flow of each character is included the idea that they are not allowed to enunciate to their interlocutors, that is, they think but do not say. On the contrary, the dialogues in relation to the other, which constitute moments of objectivity, compel a structured, coherent, and socialized thought, and they allow the reader to understand the context in which the narrative takes place.

In an exercise in transposing these two narrative planes into our daily experience, we could imagine what our thoughts would be like if we did not express them in words and did not take into account alterity (on the other, on the screen, on paper). Alterity requires coordinating in syntax and logic the ideas that flow.

His novels clearly show this contrast, these two modes of thought: whether it is the dialogue that interrupts the intimate flow of thoughts, or the reflection of thoughts that tend to move away from the dialogue with alterity. We are therefore permanently confronted with the continuous balancing of the dominant modes of thought of the schizo-paranoid position and the depressive position (SP<–>D).

As an illustration of an 'inner monologue' or 'thought flow' of the schizo-paranoid position, I select a paragraph from *Ulysses*. I chose Chapter 1, entitled *Proteus*, where Stephen Dedalus indulges in a mind-blowing 'inner monologue' while walking by the sea, a beautiful illustration of what Antonino Ferro calls "semantic nests, that is, places of discourse they keep within and other communicative possibilities" (2017, p. 180):

> "Ineluctable modality of the visible: at least that if no more, through my eyes. Signatures of all things I am here to read, seaspawn and seawrack, the nearing tide, that rusty boat. Snotgreen, bluesilver, rust: coloured signs. Limits of the diaphane. But he adds: in bodies. Then he was aware of them bodies before of them coloured. How? By knocking his sconce against them, sure. Go easy. Bald he was and a millionaire, *maestro di color sanno*. Limit of the diaphane in. Why in? Diaphane, adiaphane. If you can put your fingers through its i tis a gate, if not a door. Shut your eyes and see".

(p. 45)

It is difficult to capture Stephen Dedalus's thoughts here because they constantly change form (dispersive thinking – SP). But the first sentence of the paragraph is a quote from the Greek philosopher Aristotle that promotes the importance of vision because, according to him, the world would only exist because we see it. The sentence thus prepares the importance of the vision that is present in this text. Dedalus, wandering along the waterfront, goes on naming what he sees and wondering about the existence of what does and does not have color: "snotgreen, bluesilver, rust" (existence) and then "diaphane, adiaphane" (nonexistence), and in the end the prevalence of seeing, even with closed eyes: "shut your eyes and see" (Ulysses, p. 45).

Here we have a 'flow of consciousness', a flow of thought where one word resembles another, which suggests yet another, in a continuous movement. Of course, this is beautifully illustrated and audible due to the homophony only in the English language (see, sea). Joyce's writing is to be read and to be heard!

What could the sentence "if you can put your five fingers through its i tis a gate, if no tis a door" mean? One possible interpretation would be that of a woman's traditional method of verifying vaginal dilation: if she runs five fingers across her cervix, she will be able to give birth to her baby. This kind of sudden association seems strange, but we know that the author lived in fear that his wife would get pregnant again (Volaco, 1982).

Joyce's extraordinary wealth of mind is also related to the absence of Cartesian mind/body duality. Food, sleep, sexuality, menstruation, and all other bodily needs and functions occupy much of the thoughts of the novel's central characters. There is always a dialogue between body and mind. Some even claim that the main character of Ulysses is the human body with which language merges completely – when he eats, the language ruminates, when he masturbates, the language becomes excited, when he defecates, the language becomes disgusting, and so on. It is clearly about the ability to dream the body and its physiological functions or, in the language of the Bionian grid, to function on the "C line, which always allows the possibility of dreaming, visualizing with the mind's eyes, or the alpha function, other possibilities" (Ferro, 2017, p. 180). Two illustrations of the attempt to literarily materialize the consciousness of the body:

Stephen and Bloom end the night sharing the satisfaction of a basic need:

At Stephen's suggestion, at Blooms's instigation both, first Stephen, then Bloom, in penumbra urinated, their sides contiguous, their organs of micturition reciprocally rendered invisible by manual circumposition, their gazes, first Bloom's, then Stephen's, elevated to the projected luminous and semiluminous shadow.

(*Ulysses*, p. 825)

An inner monologue by Nora Bloom about her sexuality:

> I was learning over him with my white ricestraw hat to take the new-
> ness out of it the left side of my face the best my blouse open for his
> last day transparent kind of shirt he had I could see his chest pink he
> wanted to touch mine with his for a moment but I wouldn't let him
> he was awfully put our first for fear you never know consumption of
> leave me with a child embarazada that old servant Ines told me that
> one drop even if it got into you at all after I tried with the Banana
> but I was afraid it might break and get lost up in me somewhere
> because they once took something down out of a woman that was
> up there for years covered with line salts there they could never get
> far enough up.
>
> (*Ulysses*, p. 902)

Joyce was perhaps the novelist who pushed the literary technique of the
stream of consciousness to the extreme, by which the conventional and
omniscient outer narrator is no longer needed. Instead, the deep study of a
character's mind could influence the narrative's progress. Once, in Trieste,
early in his career as a novelist, pointing to a drunken young man who
passed by, he said, "I would like to turn to paper the thousand complexities
of your mind". And so, he took the first steps in experimental literature,
beginning to experiment with how a character's mental state can affect the
prose style. In *Ulysses*, if a character is tired, the narrative itself becomes
slurred, 'tired' – as in the episode *Eumaeus* (1922/1975, p. 637); if a character is intoxicated it is the narrative itself that becomes 'drunk' – as in
the episode *Oxen of the Sun*; if a character is dominated by visions and
hallucinations, the writing itself becomes delusional; In *A Portrait of the
Artist as a Young Man* the language develops throughout the book as the
character grows, matures, and becomes able to narrate his inner world in a
more sophisticated way. In *Ulysses*, still at the narrative level, we have the
narrative form (language) of the child, of the workers, of the single girl, of
the married lady, etc.

An interesting illustration of prose realizing that the mind is entering the
sleep state is found in *Ulysses*: when Mr. Bloom begins to fall asleep, his
mind clings to the expression "Sinbad the Sailor", but the sound overlaps
the meaning when he loses consciousness and results in

> Tinbad the Tailor and Jinbad the Jailer and Whinbad the Waler and
> Ninbad the Nailer and Finbad the Failer and Binbad the Ball Pinbad
> the Pailer and Minbad the Mailer and Hinbad the Rail the Raile Dinbad

the Kailer and Vinbad the Quailer and Linbad the Yailer and Xinbad the Phailer.

(*Ulysses*. Episode *Ithaca*, p. 871)

The interest in the workings of the human mind leads Joyce to write: "A large part of all human existence is spent in a state that cannot be made conscious by the use of awakened language, pure dry grammar, and propulsive plot". What would the unconscious sound like to him? It would certainly be a mixture (condensation) of all human languages. Joyce created a new language that somehow reproduced the dislocations, the unexpected changes of ideas, the condensations and discontinuities of dreams, with the creation of "valise words", authentic "semantic nests", in the words of Antonino Ferro, similar to the crowded speech of schizophrenics, such as the word "*riverrun*" that opens and closes the novel *A Portrait of the Artist as a Young Man*, simultaneously resubmitting to *river, run, riveranno* (find), *rêverons* (we will dream).

The continuous oscillation between dispersive and oneiric thoughts and integrative and vague thoughts (SP<—>D) is also clearly present in *Ulysses'* slow and laborious process of gestation and composition, for Joyce himself states:

> Regarding Ulysses, I write and I think and I write and I think all day long [vague mind, D] and part of the night [dream mind, SP]. It is in progress, as it has been for the past five or six years. But the ingredients will only melt [total mind and object, D] when they reach a certain temperature.
>
> (Joyce to Pound, 1975/1992, p. 426)

Finally, we cannot fail to take into account the fact that, in Joyce's narratives, the discourse is polyphonic, that is, several voices are acting. There are several monologues of the main characters, one monologue of one character interrupted by the monologue of another. At the end of the novels, almost always in the last chapter, all monologues merge into one unit, showing the wholeness of life. This feature also fits into SP<—>D: the first, whose fundamental feature is the fragmentation of being and object, the second being emphasized by the feeling of the wholeness of the self and of the object. To this style that Joyce conquered that gave him total freedom, we can call it, in Bionian terminology, "flexible continent".

Despite having been banned in Great Britain and the United States, James Joyce was eventually recognized as one of the greatest writers of the twentieth century and *Ulysses* was hailed as a masterpiece, not only on a

50   *Monologues and dialogues in Joyce's work*

literary level by the revolution he sparked in the modern novel, but also at the psychological level.

Ezra Pound (1922/2006) praised *Ulysses* as a "super novel [...] a report on the state of the human mind in the twentieth century" (cit. by Pindar, p. 48). For T.S. Eliot (1888–1965) the novel had "the importance of a scientific discovery [...] By using myth, by manipulating a continuous parallelism between contemporaneity and antiquity" – also due to the use of different levels of mental functioning from the earliest primary to the most secondary and sophisticated. For him, "*Ulysses* is the most important expression that the modern age has arranged" (Eliot, cit. by Pindar, 2004/2006). There were those who called Joyce a 'literary scientist' for his imitation and literary recreation of the mind in the dream state. Joyce himself, in his essay *The State of Tongues*, argues that "Literature is as intellectual as Mathematics and deserves to be considered as a science. Shakespeare and Milton deal with facts and ideas like any scientist" (Pindar, 2004/2006, p. 34).

We can say that, for many writers, romance as a genre is not only a mirror but also a research tool and is very close to essay, reflection, and research.

References

Bion, W. R. (1962). *Learning from experience*. London: Heineman.
Bion, W. R. (1963). *The elements of psycho-analysis*. London: Heineman.
Delgado, L. (2011). *TAT e Criatividade [Thematic apperception test and creativity]: estudo psicodinâmico*. Lisboa: ISPA – Instituto Universitário.
Ferro, A. (2017). *As Vísceras da Mente [Guts of the mind]: Silabário emocional e narrações*. Lisboa: Coisas de Ler.
Joyce, J. (1916/1964). *A portrait of an artist as a young man*. London: New Travelers Library.
Joyce, J. (1922/1968). *Ulysses*. London: The Bodley Head LTD.
Joyce, J. (1939/1975). *Finnegans wake*. London: The Trustees of the Estate of James Joyce.
Joyce, J. (1975/1992). *Selected letters of James Joyce*. London: Faber & Faber.
Klein, M. (1946/1996). Notes sur Quelques Mécanismes Schizoides [Notes on Some Schizoid Mechanisms]. In *Dévelopements de la Psychanalyse* (pp. 274–300). Paris: Presses Universitaires de France.
Lodge, D. (2002/2009). *A Consciência e o Romance* [Conscience and romance]. Lisboa: Ed. Asa.
Pindar, I. (2004/2006). *Joyce*. Lisboa: Asa.
Pound, E. (1922/2006). *Ezra Pound, um escritor modernista* [Ezra Pound, a modernist writer]. Revista Ler, 53–61. Lisboa: Fundação Círculo dos Leitores.
Volaco, G. (1982). *O Retorno da Literatura e Psicanálise* [The Return of Literature and Psychoanalysis]. Rio-de-Janeiro: Paz &Terra.

7   *Galileo Galilei*, by Bertolt Brecht, as a metaphor for the continuous transformational movement of thought

"The (in)tranquility that sustains us" could be a more suggestive, ironic, paradoxical title – in short, highly unsaturated, also linked to the uneasiness that comes from the movement and inconsistency of our thoughts and opinions.

Galileo Galilei's life, which includes the famous episode of the scientist's abjuration, is a recurring theme in the work of Brecht, who resorted to three complete versions of plays about the Italian scientist. We can say that the theme 'Galileo Galilei' traversed at least 18 years of Brecht's life (from 1938 to 1956) and that, in this time, his opinion about the character radically changed three times. Thus, we have three versions of a central and constant theme, the character Galileo. In these central pieces of Bertolt Brecht's work, written between 1938 and 1956, the German playwright chooses paradigmatic situations in Galileo's life to problematize issues that plagued the author and remain current, such as the implications of science and the scientist's relationship with society. The astronomer's experiments put into question not only the fundamental notions of science, but also the worldview and the situation of man on planet Earth (Peixoto, 1977): 1st version (1938), Danish version, Galileo = heroic figure; 2nd version (1946) American version, Galileo = criminal figure; 3rd version (1954), German version, Galileo = scoundrel figure, antisocial.

1st version: The first version of the text was written in 1938, in his exile in Denmark, when many believed in the irresistible victory of Nazism in Germany. The expectation of a barbaric era was evident, and the author used Galileo's path to address issues that disturbed him emotionally and intellectually (ideologic). Galileo appears as a man of science committed to knowing the world. He is a heroic figure, concerned with the education of the people and who, therefore, writes in vulgar Italian and not in Latin. In the end, he is a man who does not resist and retracts, for lack of strength to oppose the Inquisition. He is shattered, but he

DOI: 10.4324/9781003329015-7

spends his last days preparing new works that would do anything to cross the border and revolutionize science and the world. Brecht thus conveys to his compatriots, who live under Nazism, the idea that it is worth hiding their ideas so that they can later disseminate them (Willet, 1967).

2nd version: Written at the end of the war (1946), it is marked by the 'scandal' of the atomic bomb on Hiroshima. Brecht rethinks the responsibility of scientists, thus altering the entire end of the piece, changing the initial meaning of the text. According to the playwright, overnight, the biography of the founder of modern physics was read in a different way. Brecht writes:

> Galileo's crime is the original sin of the modern natural sciences … The atomic bomb, as a technical phenomenon and as a social phenomenon, is the classic end product of his contribution to science and his failure to society. Galileo's crime was not his retraction, his denial of scientific truth, but the fact that he has robbed science of the core of its social significance.
>
> (Brecht, cit. by Crato, 2006)

The astronomer knows the discovery of the telescope, prioritizes his personal interests above all else, disregarding the social consequences.

3rd version: This version essentially follows the previous one, but Galileo's moral condemnation is even more extreme. In this version, his figure becomes "antisocial, and must be shown as a social criminal, a scoundrel" and the scenes are written with that purpose. In one of the new scenes, for example, the astronomer regrets that he once wrote in vulgar Italian, stating that "the language of fishmongers was not appropriate for high things" (Crato, 2006).

The Portuguese adaptation of Brecht's play, *A Vida de Galileu*, that premiered in 2006 and was being shown at Teatro Aberto (Portuguese adaptation by João Lourenço and Vera San Payo), is based more on the second version of the original play, but showing a more multifaceted, more realistic, richer, less cleaved and idealized character, both positively and negatively.

Bion, in *Elements in Psychoanalysis* (1963) described a conscious activity present in the creative process consisting of the continuous oscillation between a dispersal mental state (PS) and an integrative state (D). This thought function was named PS<–>D. In the creative process, thinking involves the dismantling of previous opinions and theories, with the development of new opinions and theories. By changing the way of thinking, the continent must be dissolved before it can be reshaped, and this effort has the feeling of something 'shattering'. The Bionian process of PS<–>D, the function of thought consisting of the continuous oscillation between a dispersal mental state (PS) and a security mental state (D), is clearly visible through the constitution and destruction of three consistent and structured opinions of Brecht on Galileo.

In addition to stating ♀♂ as founding elements of mental activity, Bion (1963) also spelled out the links that can unite ♀ with ♂: H (hate), L (love), K (knowledge). O (to be read as a letter and not as a number; designates a point of origin of a truth that cannot be known, except through the products of its transformations). The bond indicates the quality of the dominant emotional experience, the basic emotion that dominates the encounter. They therefore refer to the link between the *self* and the object (Grotstein, 2007) as well as the link between internal objects (Amaral Dias, 2010).

Let us then identify the models of the meeting between Brecht's mind (♀) and the thoughts about Galileo (♂), seeking to clarify the basic emotion that presided over each of these meetings. Bion gives the greatest importance to the bonds created and, according to him, the term *bond* designates an emotional experience by which two people or two parts of the same person are related to each other. The sign K indicates normality of knowledge, desire to know oneself or another. The sign K– indicates the pathology of knowledge, absence of desire to know. L is the sign designating the bond of love. The sign H indicates hatred towards another person or a part of oneself (Bion, 1962a/1991).

We saw earlier that, in the first version (Danish), Galileo is thought of as a 'heroic figure', both as a human being and as a scientist, and it is evident that the dominant bond is L (love and admiration). As for the desire to know him, the bond K is present in its negative form, K–, as it knows only a part of the character.

In the second (American) version, corresponding to a first transformation of the continent, in which Galileo is thought of as a 'criminal figure', 'selfish', the dominant bond is clearly H (hate). The desire to know comes in the form of K– (avoidance of knowledge, Green, 2013) due to the fragmentary perception of Galileo, splitting what should not be separated.

In the third version (German), the second transformation, in which Galileo is thought of as a "despicable figure, scoundrel", the bond that presides over the union ♀♂ is K– (indifference, contempt, Grotstein, 2007).

Only in the Portuguese version (*Galileo's Life*, Teatro Aberto, 2006, Lisbon) is Galileo described with more realism, moderation, complexity and depth, that is, as a total object, with the dominant bond being K+ (desire to know), evidencing that only in this version is there a true tendency to move, to know the truth about the figure of Galileo (K → O) and that the mind is clearly in a depressive position (D).

The analysis of the three plays by the playwright Bertolt Brecht about Galileo Galilei shows us that the thoughts about that character underwent transformations and were dictated essentially by strong emotional charges, changing according to the quality of the emotions, L or H, and this finding puts us before the great and eternal question of the importance of emotions, feelings, and effects in the determination of thoughts and our opinions about people, situations, or topics important to us. The human being is a constantly changing being, and changing our minds is a part of life. As if an opinion were an emotionally invested idea. We are not the ones who have an opinion, but it is the opinion that has us.

Some illustrations of the primacy of feelings over thoughts:

- Chorus of the opera *Rigoletto* (1851) by Giuseppe Verdi

La donna è mobile	(The woman is unstable
qual pluma al vento	like a feather in the wind
muta d'acento	she changes her feelings
e di pensiero.	and thoughts.)

- António Lobo Antunes (writer): "Then we confuse the reasons why we like or dislike the piece. There are many affective elements. It is very difficult to judge. The person is mistaken for the piece, and the piece for the person. If a person is nice, I am much more likely to enjoy what they do" (Actual, 2017, p. 14–15).
- Adolf Hitler's *Mein Kampf*: It is evident that Hitler's ideological program and worldview, with its key components being the destruction of the Jewish people and the acquisition of living space at the expense of Russia, more than being a result of rationality, comes from an aversion that bordered on fixation, from a hatred so deeply entrenched that it could only have been grounded in deep fear.
- Sigmund Freud [about the impulses of aggression and hatred not having disappeared and remaining repressed in the unconscious mind, awaiting the opportunity to become active]: "Our rationality is weak and dependent on affective forces that it ignores, and we are all compelled to behave [and think] in a smart or stupid manner according to repressed emotional imperatives".

References

Amaral Dias, C. (2010). *Teoria das Transformações* [Theory of transformations]. Coimbra: Almedina.
Bion, W. (1962/1991). Uma teoria do pensar [A theory of thinking]. In Spillius (Ed.), *Melanie Klein Hoje* (Vol. 1, pp. 185–193). Rio-de-Janeiro: Imago.

Bion, W. (1963). *The elements of psycho-analysis*. London: Heineman.

Crato, N. (2006). Galileu no Palco [Galileo in stage]. *Revista Atual*. Jornal Expresso, 6 Maio, 14–15.

Green, A. (2013). *Penser la psychanalise: avec Bion, Lacan, Winnicott, Laplanche, Aulagnier, Anzieu, Rosolato* [Thinking about psychoanalysis: with Bion, Lacan Winnicott, Laplanche, Aulagnier, Anzieu, Rosolato]. Paris: Ithaque.

Grotstein, J. S. (2007). *A beam of intense darkness: Wilfred Bion's legacy to psychoanalysis*. London: Karnac.

Lobo Antunes, A. (2017). Entrevista [Interview]. *Revista Atual*. Jornal Expresso.

Peixoto, J. L. (1977). *Brecht, Vida e Obra* [Brecht, Life and Work]. Rio-de-Janeiro: Paz e Terra.

Willet, J. (1967). *O Teatro de Brecht* [Brecht's theater]. Rio-de-Janeiro: Zahar.

8 Some psychological dimensions present in the activity of creative writer and reader

From a historical perspective, the intimate writing of personal experience only emerges in the modern age, with the emergence of individualism. In the world of Greco-Roman and medieval antiquity, due to the dilution of man in the *communitas*, personal experience, private and intimate life were not worth reporting. Only the heroic and religious narratives fascinated the public. With the fall of great certainties and with the importance given to the individual, the need for introspection and the importance of the inner life intensified – Who am I? What do I feel? – This trend has grown so much that passing through the literature of the 'stream of consciousness' (Virginia Woolf, Henry James, later James Joyce …) has resulted in one of the hallmarks of the contemporary novel being a mixture of fiction and autobiography (Saul Bellow, Ernesto Vila-Matas, Julian Barnes …). On the part of the reader/receiver there has also been a significant change in the reading experience, with a much greater freedom to create new meanings to the text, depending on their wishes and personal problems.

To talk about the world and the Other, or to read about the world and the Other, is to talk and read about the world and the Other within us.

The literary work is conceived only in the pair of the creative writer/ reader, and the creative receiver, insofar as "every word implies two, one who speaks and one who listens" (Paz, 1956). In fact, the work of fiction is only really complete at the time of the reading process and, therefore, depends on the reader's creative cooperation to make it an imaginary object capable of triggering fantasies and a range of interpretations that may give personal meaning to what has just been read. We take into account the effect that a literary work can have on each reader, producing different emotions and interpretations – we are in the field of open work (Eco 1962/1989). If there is a clear intention of the writer to produce in the reader a constellation of thoughts and emotions, there is also an intention on the part of the creative reader to make his own interpretations as well as the intention of the actual text itself through the elements that constitute it. We remain in

DOI: 10.4324/9781003329015-8

the field of open work, the object of various intentions and interpretations. Just as the writer must be free to be creative in order to express his ideas and emotions, so the reader must have the necessary freedom to open up to new senses and emotions.

Most books are short lived. Only the books in which the author completely surrendered himself through the transmutation of his internal psycho-physical experiences – the 'bowels', blood, anxiety, tears, joy, excitement, semen – in ink signs/symbols through the processes of sublimation survive. The essayist and philosopher George Steiner called this process "the miracle of the sign", capable of creating an autonomous life, creating fictional characters with real emotions.

Psychoanalysis has always recognized how much the works of the great authors, with their characters, function as continents of integrated or disso-ciated aspects of the creator's personality, receiving projections and resig-nifications, thus allowing them to be reintroduced in a more integrated way (Bion, 1962/1991). The concept of personification (Klein 1926/1996) is useful for understanding the dynamic process involved in the genesis of the novel's character, and it is well known how its creation can have a balancing and protective function in the psychic dynamics of a subject. This process was initially identified in children with the construction of the 'imaginary friend' or 'double' (Klein, 1929/1996) and later Fairbairn (1944/1952) in stating that all figures that appear in dreams and fantasies are representa-tions of part of the dreamer's personality, belonging to the catalog of his inner world.

Literature tells us not only of others but of others in us, and it can be said that all fiction has autobiographical aspects, just as all autobiography has fictional aspects. The poet Rainer Maria Rilke confirms this in *Letters to a Young Poet*: "For the writer a loneliness is necessary, not in the sense of social isolation but of recollection towards himself [...] if there are terrors, those terrors are ours, if there are abysses, they are our abysses" (1929/1984, p. 8). Goethe is even clearer, referring to his novel *The Elective Affinities*: "Even in the deepest part of my book you will find allusions to lived sit-uations [and the novel] has no single line that I had not lived" (Goethe 1809/1979, p. 11). And what about Gustave Flaubert's famous apocryphal statement "Mme Bovary c'est moi", later completed by "d'après moi"? In my opinion, it refers not only to the central character of the novel, Emma Bovary, but to the whole novel, the whole composition of a completely ordered universe and, according to his personal vision as a romantic being, of love, of the dissatisfaction of desire, of the social taboos of the society in which he lived. And what of the blatant autobiographical traits present in some of Dostoevsky's great works, namely the adoration for the mother and the addiction to gambling in *The Player* (1867/2009)? Finally, let us take for illustration a novel by one of the masters of American literature, Saul Bellow's *Humboldt's Gift* (1975/2012). In fact, the novel is about Charles Citrine, a character that is easily glued to the author himself, who said that "fiction is the highest form of autobiography".

Freud writes: "[art is] a region in which the efforts of primitive man to achieve omnipotence retain their full vigor". And in *Totem and Taboo*, "it is only through art that a man consumed by desires will achieve something similar to the fulfillment of those desires, something which, thanks to artistic illusion, produces emotional effects as if it were real" (Freud, 1913/1981, p. 1804). A complement to T. S. Eliot's statement: "The human race cannot stand much reality". These statements point us to the fact that the creative writer and reader find in creation the possibility of liberating themselves from their reality/identity, that is, they may, for a moment, free themselves from the cultural, social, civilizational, sexual, temporal, geographical imprisonment in which they live by allowing them to incarnate other lives and experiences impossible to live in reality. Or by allowing them to give life to the various identities that inhabit them deeply and clandestinely. As Olga Tokarczk, Nobel laureate of Literature/2018, says in a very recent interview with a Portuguese magazine: "Romance is a great invention of humanity comparable to the most refined communication between people. It is the transmission of something communicable and much deeper that teaches us empathy. For a moment we may be someone else" (Tokarczuk, 2019, p. 18). We speak of empathy in the sense of the possibility of unveiling and feeling life through the eyes and feelings of others. And what of the relationship, the 'dialogues' that sometimes last months, years, of the author with the created characters, or the reader himself with the characters in the book?

We believe that true literature has to do with the emotional aesthetic and even spiritual revelation, with confronting complex, contradictory, sometimes even paradoxical characters, with how beings love and hurt each other and themselves. It has to do with the unexpected in the text and with expanding the knowledge and deepening of the ego on the part of both the creative writer and the creative reader. The continent and negative capacities (Bion), the epistemophilic drives, the love of truth (Klein), must be active to allow the inner plunge to meet the 'raw material' and emerge with the creation of fictional characters who possess real worldviews and emotions, whether on the part of the writer or the reader, for a deep confrontation with these characters. Let us recall characters and plots that surely compelled the creative writer/reader to venture into the abysses of their self: Shakespeare's *Macbeth* and *Hamlet*, *Anna Karenina* of Tolstoy, *Bovary* of Flaubert, *Captain Ahab* of Melville, *Leopold Bloom* of Joyce, *Adriano* and *Zeno* from Yourcenar. But creative writing can also be based on the small form, the movements of ordinary lives, the way they intertwine and deceive each other, always remaining the same, in short, the plaid of human relationships and their attractions and rejections, as with *No*a and *Theo*, the protagonist couple in the book by Israeli writer Amoz Oz, *Don't Call It Night* (1994/2019). Or the conflicts and contradictions of New York Jew *Nathan Zuckerman*, alter ego of Philip Roth.

As written previously, in fictional writing, we are fully in the realm of sublimation, that is, in the process of transforming into ordered symbols in an aesthetic order of psychophysical elements, endogenous stimuli that may also be expectant of the writer in relation to objects, or exogenous stimuli. The work is, for the creator, a way to discharge this excess. Sublimation can thus be understood as a process that tends to transform the inner world of the creative subject, ordering and appeasing it. In this case, literary work will be a source of pleasure, will have a self-therapeutic effect. This is what Janine Chasseguet Smirgel tells us in her beautiful book *Pour une Psychanalyse de l'Art et de la Créativité* (For a Psychoanalysis of Art and Creativity) about creative artwork as containing the ability to repair the damaged self: "The creative act constitutes one of the privileged modalities of reparative realization" (1977, p. 90) and, further on, "the creative act is an attempt to achieve integrity, that is, to surpass castration at all levels [...] it is to fill in by creation all the failures of maturation at all stages of development" (op. cit., p. 102).

This is the case of writer Graham Greene who, as a child, had always suffered from an anxiety–depressive syndrome (perhaps an introjective depression) and which, through the constant literary creation in which much of the work is permeated by characters tormented by moral and existential crises and that the feeling of sin is a constant – as in, for example, *The Power and Glory* (1940/1978) – had a cathartic, elaborative, and reparative role in his sense of self, perceived as damaged. Green himself claimed that writing was his therapy. In an interview with writer Amos Oz (2005), he stated that writer Paul Auster had told him that "writing is not a job for normal people, one must be damaged to write", and Oz agreed that "I live surrounded by ghosts, I talk and discuss with them, but, when I finish writing, they disappear, and in the end I never read my books" (2005).

But what works from the standpoint of literary production may not work from the self-therapeutic standpoint, sometimes leading to a worsening mental state or even suicide. Let's look at three cases:

Paul Celan's poetic work, although aesthetically magnificent, did not give him greater tranquility, psychic well-being, and did not allow him an internal elaborative process without a restorative effect, perhaps for lack of internal distancing. He writes of his writing: "transfigured language of an individual and, according to its deepest essence, present presence" (Poems,

1929/1985). In the case of Primo Levy, much of his work, especially in *If This Is a Man* (1958/2010) focuses on the description and pursuit of overly rational and reflective understanding – describe, report, interrogate Auschwitz – without true emotional expression of his traumatic experience, which may indicate a powerful defense against the highly traumatic affects. It lacked catharsis and the elaboration of emotions. Or the case of the poet and writer Charles Bukowski, who built a completely autobiographical work of literature, with marginal themes and characters. A literature without filter, raw, almost pornographic, spat out, easily provoking disgust in the reader. An evacuating literature of evil internal objects, without real reparative elaboration. Good internal objects are incarcerated and attacked by the bad objects, as in the famous *BlueBird* poem. Elucidative, the title of the publication of his collection: *Writing Not to Go Crazy* (1969/1994). Still an interesting (apocryphal) story: James Joyce, living in Zurich, and worried about his daughter Lucy's mental disorders, is said to have led her to consult the famous psychoanalyst Carl Jung, also telling him that she was trying to write, like her father. At the end of the consultation with Lucy the psychoanalyst told him: "where you swim, your daughter drowns".

The issue of emotional distance from writing and mental elaboration that we have just addressed in relation to the writer, puts us in the face of the reader's expectation. In the case of best sellers and 'soap novels', the distance may be small, because they do not require from the reading public any confrontation with the unexpected, with the unknown, with the disquieting, as there is *a priori* identification between the expectation presupposed by the text and the expectation of the reader, remaining always in its familiar comfort zone. The Freudian concept '*unheimlisch*' (uncanny) (Freud, 1919/1982) is useful and pertinent. According to Shelling, "unheimlisch is all that should have remained secret and hidden but came to light" (p. 2487). In the experience of reading, the confrontation with the 'unheimlisch' may lead the reader to refuse to continue reading, to protect himself through, for example, a mechanical reading, or, on the contrary, if his continent psychic functions are solid, tolerate the disquieting and be able to promote new meanings that were previously prevented.

Finally, we address the question of the mental dimension in which both the creative writer and the creative reader should be situated. We believe that both – the first in adherence to the character's gestation, the second in adherence to the character's reception – must be situated in what the theory of literature calls 'narrative pact', that is, the complicity that both establish with the character, pretending to believe it. The English poet Samuel Coleridge called this the need for a "temporary suspension of disbelief". In psychoanalytic terms, we could designate this process conceptualized by

Winnicott in *Playing and Reality* (1975) by activating the potential space or transitive area of the mind, that is, the ability to create a psychic dimension that is neither self nor non-self and that does not belong to the internal or external world. It is an intermediate area of experience situated between internal reality and external reality, and where the essence of the experience in this area lies not in the ability to know, but to delude oneself into believing.

References

Bellows, S. (1975/2012). *O Legado de Humboldt* [Humboldt's gift]. Lisboa: Quetzal.

Bion, W. (1962/1991). Uma teoria do pensar [A theory of thinking]. In E. B. Spillius (Ed.), *Melanie Klein Hoje* (Vol. 1, pp. 185–193). Rio-de-Janeiro: Imago.

Bukowski, C. (1969/1994). *Notas de um Velho Safado* [Notes from a dirty man]. S. Paulo: Prosa, Verso e Arte.

Celan, P. (1929/1985). *Poemas, Paul Celan* [Poems, Paul Celan]. Lisboa: Cotovia.

Dostoievski, F. (1867/2009). *O Jogador* [The player]. Lisboa: Relógio d'Água.

Eco, U. (1962/1989). *Obra Aberta* [Open work]. Lisboa: Difel.

Fairbairn, R. (1944/1952). As Estruturas Endopsíquicas Consideradas em Termos de Relação de Objeto [Endopsychic structures considered in terms of object relation]. In R. Fairbairn (Ed.), *Estudos Psicanalíticos da Personalidade* (pp. 65–107). Rio-de-Janeiro: Inter-América.

Freud, S. (1913/1981). Totem y Tabu [Totem and Taboo]. In *Sigmund Freud, Obras Completas* (Tomo II, pp. 1747–1981). Madrid: Biblioteca Nueva.

Freud, S. (1919/1981). Lo Siniestro [The 'Uncanny']. In *Sigmund Freud Obras Completas* (Tomo II, pp. 2483–2505). Madrid: Biblioteca Nueva.

Goethe, J. W. (1809/1979). *Afinidades Electivas* [Ellective affinities]. Lisboa: Relógio d'Água.

Greene, G. (1940/1970). *O Poder e a Glória* [The power and glory]. Lisboa: Livros do Brasil.

Klein, M. (1926/1996). Princípios Psicológicos da Análise de Crianças [Psychological principles of children analysis]. In *Melanie Klein – Amor, Culpa e Reparação* (pp. 153–163). Rio-de-Janeiro: Imago.

Klein, M. (1929/1996). Personificação no Brincar das Crianças [Personification in children's play]. In *Melanie Klein – Amor, Culpa e Reparação* (pp. 228–239). Rio-de-Janeiro: Imago.

Levy, P. (1958/2010). *Se Isto É Um Homem* [If this is a man]. Lisboa: Teorema.

Oz, A. (1994/2019). *Não Chames Noite à Noite* [Don't call it night]. Lisboa: Tinta da China.

Oz, A. (2005). *Entrevista a Amos Oz*. Revista Visão, 35–38.

Paz, O. (1956/1997). *El Arco y La Lira* [The bow and the lyre]. Madrid: Casa del Libro.

Rilke, E. M. (1929/1984). *Cartas a um Jovem Poeta* [Letters to a young poet]. Lisboa: Antígona.

Smirgel, J. C. (1977). *Pour une Psychanalyse de l'Art et de la Créativité* [For a psychoanalysis of art and creativity]. Paris: Gallimard.
Tokarczk, O. (2019). Entrevista [Interview]. *Revista E* – Jornal Expresso.
Winnicott, D. (1975). *Jeu et Réalité* [Playing and reality]. Paris: Gallimard.

9   Synthesis and final comments
Language of achievement

This book is a work of investigation and application of psychoanalytic concepts, as well as an attempt at reorganization and unification, in that it presents information, most of which is scattered in the works of different authors.

Starting from a desire to understand the psychic processes underlying the creative dynamics and the creative act, we postulated that these are part of an objective of protection/repair in the face of an internal threat, and that the creative dynamics comprises the mobilization of the sublimatory/symbolic capacities and continent capabilities for the psyche.

To create, then, would be to have the ability to mobilize a thought in contact with the real self, but relatively detoxified from the most intense problems, free from excessive obstacles. It is to enjoy a psychic apparatus whose operation, flexible and agile, allows circulation between the various instances, and manages to take advantage of the data of the unconscious thanks to a sufficiently permeable preconscious – the concept of the continent's function of the psyche having proved to be precious. We also removed a certainty, the defensive/restorative nature, from creativity, as we found that the mobilization of creative dynamics is, in subjects, automatically and urgently triggered by the pressing need to elaborate narcissistic fragility – to overcome flaws or defects, to overcome faults, and bridge scars.

In this way, we cannot see the creator as an individual who would have in his power, through heredity or some magical gift, extraordinary qualities. It will be someone else who, between two equally unbearable anxieties, is forced to discover a third way, that of creation. This creative outlet will always be a defense against anguish, be it death, loss, castration, or another.

As such, why not consider creativity as a normal dynamism due to the human need to overcome the paranoid–schizoid state described by Klein in *The Importance of Symbol-Formation in the Development of the Ego* (1930/1996)? In fact, for the author, creativity is a vital process for the survival and psycho-emotional development of the human baby, so it is

DOI: 10.4324/9781003329015-9

something fundamental to the life of *Homo Sapiens*. When we talk about the creative function in the new-born, we are talking about a vital function: either he finds a way to overcome his anguish through the ghost, or he will fall into psychosis or weakness. It is, therefore, the dynamic that goes from anguish to the symbol.

Taking into account creativity in its various qualities and greatness, from great creativity to the creativity of everyday life, we consider it to be the normative of our behaviors. In the event of intense distress, in the event of extreme difficulty that may cause risk of death or serious harm to the individual or the species, this creative dynamic can become, for the normal and moderately distressed subject, the privileged place where they are allowed their childish anxieties to find a solution for their survival. This dynamic must remain at their disposal throughout their life.

The conclusion we draw is as follows: whenever adaptation is impossible or insufficient, that is, whenever the subject does not find within himself an adequate answer to the problem he is confronted with, he is obliged to find an original solution, that is, to boost his creative capacity. And when we say original, we understand that this solution will be original for the individual who finds it or is going to use it. If a particular individual finds an answer for the first time and for himself, it is his creation. In the same way, whenever there is a rupture in a subject's life project and there is no way to remedy it; it is necessary to create new means, that is, new objects and new ideas that enable a new life project. Bearing in mind that creative dynamics are a defense against anguish, perhaps we can better understand the reason that leads certain creators to look for insecurity, be it material or emotional (loneliness, problematic relationships, drugs, alcohol, etc.), intending to create, in a way, favorable conditions for the activation of their creative process. As if anything that can exacerbate anguish should automatically increase the need to create. Let us remember, in relation to this, the words of the Italian poet Eugénio Montale (2004): "Only the isolated speak, only the isolated communicate [...] the others repeat, echo".

From a theoretical point of view, from the unified but diverse psychoanalytic universe, we highlight the presence of elements of complementarity between the three psychoanalytical concepts used in this work, imposing an intra and inter theories procedure. An illustrative example is the use of Bion's theory of the *alpha function* (1962a/1991, 1962b/1979), which integrates the three psychoanalytical models used and proves to be extremely important to understand the reason why the most qualified subjects for the creative realization are more apt for the sublimation derivation and for the elaboration of the depressive position: in fact, the role of the alpha function is paramount in creativity insofar as it is up to it to register and elaborate lived experiences, transforming into alpha elements (elements of psychic

character, sublimated) the sensory and emotional data (beta elements), leading them to consciousness, and susceptible of being thought by the device to
think thoughts and have an ego-repairing function.

Both art and science have common origins, through explosions of creativity, both seeking to provide aesthetic and comprehensive representations
of worlds beyond appearances. A great work of art, as well as a scientific
theory, represents a profound insight expressed in an effective language
– the *language of achievement*, according to Wilfred Bion (1970/1973) –
which allows a community to share and elaborate reached meanings, transforming themselves. This concept was conceived by Bion in order to rectify
problems he encountered in his analytic experiences with analysands to
other analysts. He seems to be saying that ordinary language is unsuitable
for use in psychoanalysis. The same in art or literature. The *language of
achievement* acts like a photography snapshot to extract a numinous idea or
an object from the mystic stream and capture it forever, thereby arresting its
vitality and motion. In using the artist as a model, Bion considers the final
products of the great artist. He states that the end product effected by an artist communicates a universal and lasting emotional experience in the greatest number of people in whom he intends to produce it (Bion, 1970/1973).

Some illustrations:

"*Where there is id, there must be ego*". Freud and his synthetic formula of
a therapeutic and civilizational project, that is, where repression and the
unknown are, there must be freedom and the known, consisting essentially
in the awareness of repressed sexual forces, inducing neurotic states.

The image with a soundtrack that traveled the world: Rostropovich
ecstatically playing a Bach suite, his back to the rubble of the Berlin Wall.
There, when the maximum symbol of the regime, from which he declared
himself dissident, collapsed to the sound of a perfect chord, the cellist had
what few attain, language of achievement.

Albert Einstein in his fifth article in the *Annals of Physics* (1905) – "Does
a body's inertia depend on its energy content?" – contains his famous equa-
tion (prototype of the language of achievement): $E=mc^2$ (mass is equivalent
to energy and vice versa).

Franz Kafka and his great intuitions of the totalitarian forces that were
knocking at the door, and the vision of a monstrous symbiosis between
power and slave.

Guernica (Picasso, 1937): this painting is a declaration against war and
a manifesto against violence. Besides being an undisputable icon of the
Spanish Civil War, it is nowadays a universal symbol of anti-militarism and
the struggle for human freedom.

Finally, we can synthetize our concept of creativity and creation, combining the three dimensions mentioned, stating that the great human achievements in the field of aesthetic creation and scientific discoveries are unique, original productions, the result of inventions of symbols and symbolic networks, through works of transformation based on the materials rooted in the depths of the creator's being and on the materials that the world offers him and are determined by the need to overcome the painful, the difficult, the ugly, the bad, the disharmonious, the defective, of himself and of the outside.

We finish with one of the classic Greek expression: '*Nous poietikos*'. Aristotle said that we are active, creative, poetic intelligences. And for Holderling, "*Poetically, man inhabits the Earth*". In fact, the human being lives with a type of thought that combines reason, emotion, and fantasy. "To live in relation with your feet on the ground and your head on the moon to dream", in the words of the psychoanalyst master Coimbra de Matos.

That which we call poetry – or art in general – is just an exemplary case of the creative, humble, and grandiose power that takes place in each of the mental activities. As it is an expansion of common faculties, we took artistic creation as an example so that, with its excessive exaggeration, it would also allow us to make the normal clear. What we have said about the normal creative process is valid for this rare artistic (or scientific) creative activity that is the great art, and vice versa, only to different degrees. The dancer builds his superior grace and agility out of ordinary agility. The athletic muscle is made up of a muscle that is not athletic. The great novelist builds his works from the writing and imagination capacity common to all human beings.

In short, great creativity is built on the creativity common to all human beings.

References

Bion, W. (1962a/1991). Uma teoria do pensar [A theory of thinking]. In E. B. Spillius (Ed.), *Melanie Klein Hoje* (Vol. 1, pp. 185–193). Rio-de-Janeiro: Imago.

Bion, W. R. (1962b/1979). *Aux Sources de L'Expérience* [Learning from experience]. Paris: PUF.

Bion, W. R. (1970/1973). *Atenção e Interpretação* [Attention and interpretation]. Rio-de-Janeiro: Imago.

Klein, M. (1930/1996). A Importância da Formação de Símbolos no Desenvolvimento do Ego [The importance of symbol formation in ego developement]. In *Melanie Klein – Amor, Culpa e Reparação* (pp. 387–412). Rio-de-Janeiro: Imago.

Montale, E. (2004). *Poesia. Eugénio Montale* [Poetry. Eugenio Montale]. Lisboa: Assírio e Alvim.

Index